101 Marvelous Morsels of Maternal Wisdom
—From Moms to Their Celebrity-To-Be Children

"You've got to go into engineering; that's where the money is, man."

—Maud Ariel McKoy Powell to son, Colin

"When you do good, do it unobtrusively, as if you are tossing a pebble into the sea."

—Drana Bojaxhiu to her daughter Ganxhe, known today as Mother Teresa

"Most important was to bring up the oldest one the way you want them all to go. If the oldest one comes in and says good night to his parents or says his prayers in the morning, the younger ones think that's the thing to do and they will do it."

—Rose Kennedy on son, John Fitzgerald

"I always felt like God made Muhammad special but I don't know why God chose me to carry this child. . . . He had confidence in himself and that gave me confidence in him. . . . The important thing was that he had a belief in God."

—Odessa Clay on son, Muhammad Ali

ELSA HORNFISCHER, a registered nurse and stained glass artist, is a graduate of Hartford Hospital School of Nursing and the University of Massachusetts. DAVID HORNFISCHER is the vice president of administration and finance at Berklee College of Music in Boston and a freelance writer. He is a graduate of Trinity College in Hartford and has an MBA from the University of Massachusetts. They have each had mothers for over fifty years, and Elsa has been a mother of two children for almost thirty.

Mother
Knew
Best

Wit and Wisdom from the Moms of Celebrities

Elsa and David Hornfischer

A PLUME BOOK

PLUME
Published by the Penguin Group
Penguin Books USA Inc., 375 Hudson Street, New York, New York 10014, U.S.A.
Penguin Books Ltd, 27 Wrights Lane, London W8 5TZ, England
Penguin Books Australia Ltd, Ringwood, Victoria, Australia
Penguin Books Canada Ltd, 10 Alcorn Avenue, Toronto, Ontario, Canada M4V 3B2
Penguin Books (N.Z.) Ltd, 182–190 Wairau Road, Auckland 10, New Zealand

Penguin Books Ltd, Registered Offices:
Harmondsworth, Middlesex, England

First published by Plume, an imprint of Dutton Signet,
a division of Penguin Books USA Inc.

First Printing, May, 1996
1 3 5 7 9 10 8 6 4 2

REGISTERED TRADEMARK—MARCA REGISTRADA

ISBN 0-452-27618-7

CIP data is available.

Printed in the United States of America
Set in Palatino
Designed by Jesse Cohen

this book is dedicated

To the mothers
who brought life
to these pages

They did the best they could
with what they had
and it made a difference

To our mothers
Doris and Grace
for over one century
of devotion

To the women
close to us

Amy Elsa, Sharon Grace,
and
Lum

They make a difference

ACKNOWLEDGEMENTS

When you have a son who is a literary agent, it is dangerous to suggest an idea for a book. This book started over lunch in December 1994 at a historic old Victorian inn in Llano, Texas—in fact, over a house special of a burger with peanut butter. As we lunched we discussed book ideas with our Texan literary-agent son Jim, who had just received a contract to compile a book entitled *Right Thinking*, a compendium of conservative thought through the ages.

Perhaps inspired by our interest in Dorothy Letterman's appearances on her son's *Late Show* or the flak surrounding Congressman Gingrich's mom's slightly X-rated comments about Hillary Clinton, we conceived the idea of a book about mothers of celebrities. It might have ended there. However, Jim quickly said, "That is too good of an idea not to do something about." He then added, "I'm going to bug you guys until this gets done." He was true to his word and at the risk of disappointing our son, we dutifully, and perhaps skeptically, dove into some preliminary research. We were immediately struck by the variety and depth of the material that we found from poring through biographies and watching Jack Perkins's nightly *Biography* show on the Arts and Entertainment Network. We were quickly convinced that this was indeed a project worth doing. With some editorial assistance from Jim, a proposal was soon developed with twenty short entries.

The idea found a receptive eye in Danielle Perez, editor at Dutton Signet. After much research, discussion with, and input from Jim and Danielle, we have created this book.

We have thoroughly enjoyed working together, researching and assembling these wonderful stories that truly illustrate seven essential values imparted to the future celebrities by their moms. The stories are timeless. The variety of celebrities is broad and the values are those that any parent should think about in raising their child. These stories demonstrate what the impact can be when Mom's efforts work.

We certainly have been guided by our own moms: Dave's devoted mother, Grace Hornfischer, gave him a sense of perspective to see that ideas like this can work, and Elsa's mother, Doris Bozenhard, instilled in her daughter a sense of responsibility and self-discipline to keep the project on track. Our daughter, Amy, provided ready humor at crucial times, and along with her brother, Jim, serve as living examples of our own parental efforts. We have been aided by our son-in-law, Marcel Michaud, who had the ambition to get a job in the computer business, to sell us our Power Macintosh computer, and to provide us with technical assistance. Finally, our young grandson Jacob Marcel Michaud inspired us and gave us renewed faith in the importance of effective parenting.

We also wish to acknowledge the support of the Framingham Public Library and our local bookstores which provided much of the source material for this effort. They must wonder why we read so many biographies each week!

INTRODUCTION

Mothers: All of us had one. She knew us best. Mother was there when we uttered our first cry of life, and in turn often spoke the first words we ever heard. As we grew, she would tell us much, much more: little guiding thoughts passed along to help us through a hard day. Gentle rebukes. Statements of praise. Many of her words stuck solidly in our subconscious and became, over time, the center of our moral core.

The motherly role takes on increasing interest when the child in question becomes a celebrity, for we are ever eager for new tidbits about today's and yesterday's headliners. Confronted with a proliferation of spin-savvy press agents, PR strategists, and other handlers, we grow all the hungrier for genuine, unadulterated insights into the objects of our fascination. Who better to fill this need than Mom?

Certainly Franklin Delano Roosevelt was molded by a strong and caring mother. She moved to Boston to be closer to her son at Harvard. Garry Wills's book on leadership, *Certain Trumpets*, discusses her formative influence in conjunction with FDR's executive style.

In tribute to Rose Kennedy, son Jack once said, "There's no way you can prepare for the presidency. The only things I ever learned from anybody that might have helped were some of the early things I learned from my mother." A similar tribute came from Sigmund Freud, who, commenting on the life of the German poet Goethe, noted that "sons who succeed in life have been the favorite children of good mothers."

In the following pages, we have attempted to shed light on the roles that mothers have played in famous people's lives and in doing so, illustrate critical virtues imparted by each mother to her subsequently successful offspring. The book's one hundred and one entries are organized into seven different sections, each demonstrating a particular virtue illustrated by the mother's words and actions. *Webster's New Collegiate Dictionary* defines virtue as "a moral quality conceived as a good." We have not chosen to focus on the religious or nationalistic aspects of morality but instead on those aspects of motherhood that illustrate the importance of one of these seven virtues in the life of someone who turned out to be a celebrity. These virtues underlie what became values imparted by mothers to their children.

While no person is perfect, and we certainly know all too well many of the shortcomings of our heroes, we have tried to select celebrities whom we feel have passed the test of time, have accomplished something significant in their field, were guided by the values imparted by their mothers, and who became models we might wish to emulate in some aspect of our own lives.

Our chosen virtues, which are further described in the introductions to each section, include: Ambition, Courage, Devotion, Faith, Perspective, Responsibility, and Self-discipline. This choice was difficult, but as we evaluated the relationships between many mothers and their famous children, we found such a consistent pattern of motherly influence that the categories virtually selected themselves.

This book demonstrates these virtues in action in real-life situations involving people whose lives and characteristics are well known to all. We hope you will share our pleasure in the marvelous diversity of celebrities included here. Some are current pop-culture heroes, while others date back to much earlier times. These individual stories fall together into a beautiful composite portrait of the positive impact a mother can have on a child. That mothers as far removed from one another as Maud Powell, the mother of Colin Powell, and Kate Keller, who raised writer Helen Keller, both imparted to their children a strong sense of ambition shows how such a virtue readily crosses lines of both culture and time.

This book does not attempt to say that to become successful one must have a mother with an explicit moral message. In fact, in our research we encountered many examples of those who succeeded despite problematic childhoods and difficult family situations. Once in a while adverse conditions can bring out the best in children by showing them how not to run their lives. We aim to celebrate the beneficial influence of loving and effective mothers in their children's (albeit well-known ones) lives.

While each of our stories is interesting by itself, when viewed together they serve to illustrate the importance of a positive motherly influence. If any of these stories inspire but

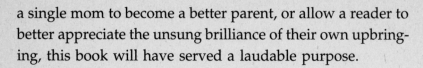

a single mom to become a better parent, or allow a reader to better appreciate the unsung brilliance of their own upbringing, this book will have served a laudable purpose.

Elsa and Dave Hornfischer
November 1995

Mother Knew Best

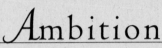

Ambition

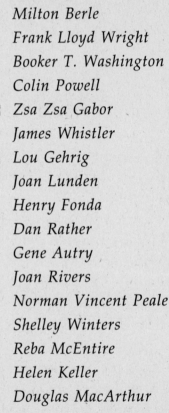

Milton Berle

Frank Lloyd Wright

Booker T. Washington

Colin Powell

Zsa Zsa Gabor

James Whistler

Lou Gehrig

Joan Lunden

Henry Fonda

Dan Rather

Gene Autry

Joan Rivers

Norman Vincent Peale

Shelley Winters

Reba McEntire

Helen Keller

Douglas MacArthur

Ambition

Mothers often encourage their children to make something of themselves, to study hard, to practice more and not give up. Mothers go to recitals, art exhibits, and praise their children's music and art. They gently nudge, guide, or at the extreme, push their children toward what they feel will make their children ambitious and therefore, a success. Ambition is a strong desire for attainment. It's often called drive, eagerness, energy, spirit, or aspiration. In the illustrations that follow, there was an ambitious mother behind the future celebrity, encouraging, facilitating, generally supporting, or even sometimes effectively questioning her child's efforts.

In some cases a mother tries to facilitate for her child what she has been unable to accomplish herself. It was Sarah Berlinger who originally wanted to be in show business, but she knew that pursuing this career would bring great shame to her family. Through her lifelong support for her son, later known as Milton Berle, Sarah achieved in a different way the success she was unable to obtain on her own, and in the process lived a long, happy life while basking in the success, appreciation, and ambition of a loving son.

A mother sometimes decides for herself what her child's ambition and goal should be, and only later finds that yes, her child is ambitious and is pursuing a goal, but neither her ambition nor her goal, but instead one of his own. Sometimes this doubting mother stimulates her offspring to prove to her that success can be achieved in the child's own way. This is a theme that appears in several of our examples. Young James Whistler practiced his art before a doubting mother who considered his gift of drawing only an "amusement." However, once she realized that he was not going to be happy until he made art his career, she supported him in every way she could. The reward? James Whistler's portrait of his mother, popularly titled *Whistler's Mother*, is one of the best-known paintings of an American artist. Similarly, a young Lou Gehrig played baseball at Columbia against his mother's wishes that he put his efforts into more scholarly goals. Colin Powell declared engineering his major at the City College of New York to please his mother, while dedicating most of his efforts and attention to his military officer–training courses.

Other examples reveal that a mother has ignited her child's ambition by her own self-sacrifice or perception of society's limitations. Young Booker T. Washington was driven to learn to read by his mother's lament that reading was "white folks' business." Katie Keller insisted that her handicapped daughter Helen get the kind of education, assistance, and support she would need to overcome her physical handicaps.

Whether these mothers shared the steering wheel of life with the child or played the role of the doubting back-seat driver, they showed that they cared, had expectations, and ultimately valued their child's achievements. It is the child who effectively understands and processes most of these verbal and nonverbal maternal messages, regardless of the mother's style in the delivery of the message, who goes on to develop the drive, energy, and ambition needed for success.

FAMOUS CHILD:	**Milton Berle**
MOTHER'S NAME:	**Sarah Glantz Berlinger**
MAMA SAID:	*"I'm glad you're a star, Milton, I was getting tired."*

Milton Berle enjoyed tremendous support from his mother in the early days of his career, and it may have been due to her own lack of the same. Though she had long aspired to become an actress, she was held back by her parents, who feared, as Berle wrote in his memoirs, that if their daughter entered show business, "she'd bring undying shame to the family name; Glantzes everywhere would have to jump off bridges."

As a result, Mrs. Berlinger fulfilled her own ambitions as she watched her son make his name. Uncle Miltie wrote, "If I hadn't succeeded, she probably would have had another kid when she was sixty and given it dancing lessons."

In his autobiography, Berle states: "Mama was with me for almost every performance I did during her lifetime, and there was so much written about her and me that people who have never met her think of her as all the stage mothers in the world wrapped into one."

SOURCES:

Milton Berle, *B.S. I Love You* (New York: McGraw-Hill, 1988).

Haskel Frankel, *Milton Berle: An Autobiography with . . .* (New York: Delacorte Press, 1974).

This motherly quote, made at the time of Wright's birth in 1876, was noted by the renowned architect in his autobiography as an example of his mother's strong impact on his life, which was marked by boundless energy, an insatiable appetite for experience, and limitless belief in his own rightness. It is not surprising that Wright grew up from childhood with the idea that there was nothing so sacrosanct as an architect's work.

Wright biographer Meryle Secrest wrote that Anna's

fierce love for her son is almost legendary. Her son was her prince and she believed both that his birth was prophesied and his career predestined.

His Wales-born mother indoctrinated him into the rich tradition of Celtic fairy tales and pagan myths. This led Wright to later name one of his own classically designed homes "Taliesin," after a Welsh poet-prophet, magician, and supernatural being who, having been made privy to supernatural knowledge, was said to have been destined for death and rebirth.

SOURCE:
Meryle Secrest, *Frank Lloyd Wright: A Biography* (New York: Alfred A. Knopf, 1992).

FAMOUS CHILD:	Booker T. Washington
MOTHER'S NAME:	Jane Washington
MAMA SAID:	*"Reading books is white folks' business."*

ane Washington, a slave of the Burroughs family, worked long hours and, according to biographer Louis R. Harlan, was "distraught by overwork and ill health," leaving her little time for Booker's upbringing. Her difficult life gave her little hope of attaining educational goals for either herself or her intelligent son. Booker had no formal schooling himself; he carried the books of his young mistress only as far as the school door, having learned at an early age that for a young black child to go inside was dangerous and, according to his mother, Jane Washington, was "white folks' business." But this prohibition fueled in him a burning ambition. "From that moment," Booker T. Washington resolved, "I should never be satisfied until I learned what this dangerous practice was like."

Booker had the task at mealtimes in the master's house of fanning flies from the table. He pulled the rope of an elaborate pulley contraption that worked a set of paper fans which, according to Harlan, beyond allowing him to demonstrate his vocational skills, permitted him to be present at dinner and thereby learn something of table manners and mealtime conversation. Booker's keen sense of observation while performing this task taught him that there was a world beyond the plantation. His determination to read, fostered by both the limitations of his mother's life and her initial warning, led him to become focused in his desire for an education.

Born in a Virginia log cabin in 1856, Booker T. Washington lived to become an educator at the Tuskegee Institute in Alabama, and a nationally respected intellectual and leader in a time of extreme racism in the United States. He was invited to the White House by President Theodore Roosevelt in recognition of his efforts.

SOURCE:
Louis R. Harlan, *Booker T. Washington: The Making of a Black Leader, 1856–1901* (New York: Oxford University Press, 1972).

FAMOUS CHILD:	Colin Powell
MOTHER'S NAME:	Maud McKoy Powell
MAMA SAID:	*"You've got to go into engineering; that's where the money is, man."*

*P*owell recalled that "I went to college for a single reason, my parents expected it." The dutiful son further complied with his parents' advice by declaring engineering as his major at the City College of New York. Powell subsequently changed his major to geology but put his primary focus on the Reserve Officer Training Corps, where he was designated a Distinguished Military Graduate.

After he had accepted his second lieutenant's commission and departed on a Greyhound bus, his mother was heard saying to her departing son, "Do your three years, come home, we'll get a job, we'll be all right." Powell's biographer, David Roth, claims it was his frugal mother, a Jamaican immigrant, who "pressed her son to achievement and success," even if it wasn't as an engineer.

Years later, when Powell was promoted to general, he modestly informed his mother with the words, "Today the President said that I actually get to be a general." Roth observed that "After twenty-one years in uniform, Maud Powell concluded that although her son had left his engineering major and was a career officer instead, everything was going to be all right."

SOURCE:
David Roth, *Sacred Honor: Colin Powell, the Inside Account of his Life and Triumphs* (New York: HarperCollins, 1993).

FAMOUS CHILD:	Sari Zsa Zsa Gabor
MOTHER'S NAME:	Jolie Gabor
MAMA SAID:	*"Any girl was a pariah—be she a princess or beggar—unless she married a rich man."*

*Z*sa Zsa recalls in her biography that she and her sister Eva grew up in a wealthy family where money was never an issue but intelligence and achievement were. Their mother felt her children were born to be queens and empresses, to marry the crème de la crème, and to personify perfection.

Zsa Zsa remembers that when she was twelve, her mother, after seeing the Prince of Wales and Mrs. Simpson at a Ritz Hotel beauty parlor, sent a letter to Buckingham

Palace suggesting that the Prince should consider "marrying her tiny daughter Zsa Zsa when she comes of age." The independent Zsa Zsa had other ideas. After her mother had discovered her youthful infatuation with the coal delivery-man and chided her, claiming she would "come to a bad end," Zsa Zsa states that she made up her mind to "spend the rest of my life proving her wrong."

That she eventually did by appearing in more than seventy films and on innumerable television programs as well as with presidents and the rich and famous in about every setting imaginable. She has had nine husbands and, as she proudly states in her book, "escaped the Nazis, outwitted Communists, defied millionaires and tycoons, captivated movie stars and moguls, and have remained fearless in the face of all manner of intimidation and danger."

She dedicated her biography to her mother, who celebrated her ninetieth birthday in 1991, calling her "the most brilliant and wonderful mother anyone could have."

SOURCE:
Zsa Zsa Gabor with Wendy Leigh, *One Lifetime Is Not Enough* (New York: Delacorte Press, 1991).

FAMOUS CHILD:	James McNeill Whistler
MOTHER'S NAME:	Anna McNeill Whistler
MAMA SAID:	*"I told him his gift had only been cultivated as an amusement, and that I was obligated to interfere or his application would confine him more than we approved."*

*J*ames McNeill Whistler, the son of Major Whistler and his wife Anna, was born in 1834 in Lowell, Massachusetts, where his father was employed as an engineer of locks and canals which served the textile industry there.

According to biographer Hesketh Pearson, although Anna was delighted that James could derive so much pleasure from his pencil, she "did not encourage such secular enjoyments." She dearly wished that like his father, he would go to West Point (which he subsequently did but lasted only three years before withdrawing) or become an engineer (he tried but always arrived late to work or not at all). When James stated flatly that he "intended to study Art in Paris," the entire family, including his mother, finally agreed, for as early as the age of two, he would crawl under his mother's dressing table with a paper and pencil while explaining, "I'se drawrin."

In 1859, Whistler moved to London where he was to stay and pursue his art for the rest of his life, as a man who, according to biographer Hesketh Pearson, "even in an age of eccentrics was considered unique." According to Leslie Albrecht Popiel of *The Christian Science Monitor*, "Perhaps no other artist's mother was so well known: *Arrangement in Grey and Black: Portrait of the Painter's Mother*, universally known as *Whistler's Mother*, is one of the most recognized paintings by an American artist."

SOURCES:

Hesketh Pearson, *The Man Whistler* (New York: Taplinger Publishing Co., 1978).

Leslie Albrecht Popiel, "Exhibits Recall Whistler's Forgotten Career," *Boston Globe*, 11 June 1995.

*L*ou, the only surviving child of Heinrich and Christina Gehrig, was born in 1903 in the poor Yorkville section of Manhattan in a neighborhood of German and Hungarian immigrants. Heinrich was not able to earn a steady living so it was up to Christina to scrub, wash, clean, cook, and take in laundry to support her family. Christina worked hard to see that her only son would have a better life—and one way to do this was to go to college. Baseball, however, continued to dominate young

Lou's life throughout childhood and even while in college. Christina steadfastly believed that baseball "was a bunch of nonsense" and "a game for bummers" for it kept young Lou from his studies, and therefore, possibly from success.

Lou eventually graduated from Columbia after continuing to play baseball on Columbia's South Field against his mother's better judgment. Lou converted his mother's ambition for him into one for himself—creating a foundation for a legendary baseball career. After signing with the New York Yankees, Lou played in 2,130 consecutive games before he retired prematurely from baseball, bravely facing death in 1941 at thirty-eight years of age from ALS, known ever since as "Lou Gehrig's disease."

SOURCE:
Ray Robinson, *Iron Horse: Lou Gehrig in His Time* (New York: W. W. Norton and Co., 1990).

FAMOUS CHILD:	Joan Lunden
MOTHER'S NAME:	Gladyce Somervill Blunden
MAMA SAID:	*When Joan was in grammar school, her friends would say, "Boy, Joanie, you're so lucky to live in that house by the airport." Joan's mother instructed her to answer, "Yes, and the harder my father works, the luckier I get."*

*J*oan Lunden (name changed from Blunden) has been seen on *Good Morning America* since 1980, interviewing some of the most famous people in the world.

She grew up during the 1950s in the upper-middle-class community of Fair Oaks, a small suburb northeast of Sacramento, California. Joan's father, a surgeon, died suddenly in a plane crash in 1964 when she was a teenager, leaving her mother to form the family into a threesome that would, in her words, "have to fight the world together." Joan went on to do well in school, to enter beauty contests, play in piano recitals, take dancing lessons, lead the local parade, and graduate from high school a year early at the age of sixteen. "Mother," Joan said, "has always valued the 'seekers' and the 'achievers' and those who dream of a better life. I know, she has said to me a thousand times, 'Hitch your wagon to a star, baby doll.' "

Joan dedicated her book to her mother who "not only gave me my start in life, but for her love and for encouraging me always to reach for the stars."

SOURCE:
Joan Lunden with Ardy Friedberg, *Good Morning, I'm Joan Lunden* (New York: G. P. Putnam's Sons, 1986).

FAMOUS CHILD:	Henry Jaynes Fonda
MOTHER'S NAME:	Herberta Fonda
MAMA SAID:	*"Do me a favor, Henry. Do Brando's on the line. Just listen to her."*

*B*orn in 1905 in Grand Island, Nebraska, Henry Fonda spent most of his life in Omaha with his parents and two sisters in a close, extended family of Christian Scientists. His pleasant childhood was intertwined with memories of playing cops and robbers, going to ball games, and attending summer camp and large family picnics along the "bumpy, dirt roads and wooden sidewalks" of Omaha. Young Henry, "devoted to his mother and sisters and in constant awe and admiration of his father," went on to become an Eagle Scout and then an underclassman at the University of Minnesota. After two years, he dropped out of college, not able to find a purpose or goal in life within the confines of a classroom.

After school ended, Henry's mother continued to exhibit her lifelong ambition and support for her son by coaxing him to try out for the Community Playhouse. The 1925 season was about to start and the company needed a juvenile actor. It was his mother's advice to listen to her friend Do Brando, the founder of Omaha's Community Playhouse and mother of infant Marlon Brando, that led Henry to the tryout and his subsequent part in a play at the Community Playhouse. Young Henry Fonda got the job, was "too self-conscious to say I didn't want to do it, or that I didn't know how to do it," and spent the rest of his life in the acting profession.

SOURCE:
Henry Fonda as told to Howard Teichman, *Fonda: My Life* (New York: New American Library/Times Mirror, 1981).

*D*an was born in oil country northwest of Houston in a small, poor town called Heights Annex, where there were unpaved streets, one general store, and "self-sufficiency was taken for granted." "Father ruled the family and work ruled father," Dan added, describing his hard-working and physically tough father— a "pipeliner" who dug ditches in which to lay pipe for the oil fields.

Through the years, Dan's mother held various jobs—

selling encyclopedias, waitressing, answering phones, sewing in a small factory and at home, making slipcovers and upholstery on a "treadle sewing machine to assist in support of the family." Dan describes her as having "remarkable energy and a strong work ethic," while making sure "her children had a better life"—all done from a home it was said was "so small you had to go outside to change your mind!"

Veda's description of the young visitor who "had a college degree" has been long remembered by her son, who doesn't remember who the visitor was, but "never forgot Mother's words or her reverent tone of voice." Although the message was an indirect one, it was very clear to Dan that to obtain a college degree was going to be a very worthy goal. Veda's hard work throughout Dan's early years demonstrated as well a clear philosophy of ambition which Dan went on to use while struggling to play football, to attain a college education, and to do the work necessary to achieve success in broadcasting.

About his mother, Dan writes, "family failures weren't failures. They were setbacks, perhaps heavy losses, disappointments, but temporary" and one "never gives up—you don't just quit. This continues to be my rule as a reporter." With a "love of words" begun in his childhood at his mother's knee and an example of ambition demonstrated by his mother, Dan catapulted his career of words into the major anchor-news position he holds today.

SOURCE:
Dan Rather with Peter Wyden, *I Remember* (Boston: Little, Brown and Co., 1991).

FAMOUS CHILD:	Orvon Gene Autry
MOTHER'S NAME:	Elnora Ozmont Autry
MAMA SAID:	*"You go to Chicago, Gene, there might not be a next time."*

*J*ust a few days before she died of cancer, Gene Autry's mother advised her soon-to-be-famous "singing cowboy" son not to miss a singing opportunity in Chicago. "If she was dying, she didn't let on," Autry noted later. He added that it was his mother who always encouraged his interest in music and wanted her oldest son to be, as she put it, "a professional man, anything other than a farmhand or a cattle trader."

Autry, whose family were ranch hands in rural Tioga,

Texas (an Autry died at the Alamo) stated that he always regarded the death of his mother at age forty-five to have been a "tragedy because I was on the verge of making the kind of money that might have prolonged her life." She never got to see her son in the ninety-five Western movies he made or see the ranches he owned.

While she supported his efforts to better himself, Autry added that like many mothers who have concerns about their children's future, she had the typical motherly nervousness about her son's artistic pursuits. He remembered that the last question she asked him before her death was whether he was sure he should quit his job with the railroad to pursue his music. However, Autry made good use of his railroad job in pursuit of a career. Armed with the free railroad pass provided by that job, a hundred and fifty dollars, and advice from Will Rogers to go to New York to try radio, Autry took his songs East before becoming one of the movies' first Western heroes during the 1950s.

SOURCE:
Gene Autry with Mickey Herskowitz, *Back in the Saddle Again* (New York: Doubleday and Co., 1978).

*T*he family home in Larchmont, New York, was a place of retreat for Joan in between auditions and performances. It was during one of these respites after a failed audition that Joan's mother gave her this advice. Beatrice Molinsky knew already what those in charge of Joan's early auditions didn't know, that Joan Rivers was to become extraordinarily successful in her career.

Throughout Joan's formative years, her mother had groomed her and her sister to live and entertain well, to go to the best colleges, to attract the "perfect upper-class boys into the perfect WASP marriages." It soon became apparent, however, that Joan had show business in her blood and would not conform. "My independence," Joan said, "was to her a rejection of her most deeply held values and became a battleground between us." Joan added, however, that in spite of this, "I found out I had a champion who believed in me, who would slug it out for me, who really loved me."

SOURCE:
Joan Rivers with Richard Meryman, *Enter Talking* (New York: Delacorte Press, 1986).

FAMOUS CHILD:	Norman Vincent Peale
MOTHER'S NAME:	Anna Peale
MAMA SAID:	*"You've got to love life; you've got to read everything, study everything, be interested in everything. You've got to be citizens of the world."*

$\mathcal{A}$nna Peale kindled Norman's ambition with stories, fairy tales, and poetry, highlighting stories of boys who rose from obscurity to become great men. Anna, very devout and strong-willed, continually prayed that young Norman would become a man of the cloth, exclaiming while viewing infant Norman in his christening gown that "he looks like a bishop already!" Inevitably, Norman Vincent Peale's ambition was stirred. Biographer Arthur Gordon continues, "In response to his mother's urging, the image of himself as a person of ultimate importance began to take shape in his mind."

Norman Vincent Peale went on to inspire countless thousands to make themselves better people with books such as *The Power of Positive Thinking*, through his magazine *Guideposts*, and in his own ministry at Marble Collegiate Church in New York City.

SOURCE:
Arthur Gordon, *Norman Vincent Peale: Minister to Millions* (New York: Prentice-Hall, 1958).

FAMOUS CHILD:	**Shelley Winters (Shirley Schrift)**
MOTHER'S NAME:	**Rose Winter Schrift**
MAMA SAID:	*"Baby, it's time you let me go. Don't forget you're an artist. You did it for both of us. Now I have to go join My Partner."*

$\mathcal{R}$ose Winter Schrift, Shelley's mother, with her "beautiful coloratura soprano," once won a St. Louis Municipal Opera contest and was offered a fully financed singing career in Italy. Rose's parents, however, had spent "all their resources getting away from the old country, and they weren't about to let their beautiful red-haired daughter go back under any circumstances," related Shelley. Rose, instead of pursuing her own career in music, married Jonas Schrift, a man picked by her parents in the custom of the "old country," and gave birth to two daughters.

With dreams of becoming a millionaire, Jonas moved the young family to Brooklyn and opened a haberdashery shop, only to see his dreams go up in smoke one Christmas right in the middle of the Depression. Because Jonas had five thousand dollars worth of insurance, the authorities were convinced that the fire was arson. Rose Schrift spent the next year courageously picking up the pieces of their lives; she worked ten- to twelve-hour days, did her best to raise the girls, moved to a cheaper apartment over a relative's butcher shop, carried on her legal battles with the State of New York, and visited her husband at Sing Sing. Finally, a new trial exonerated Jonas Schrift, but the damage had been done. His dreams of success had been destroyed.

Rose Winter Schrift watched as her daughter wrote a play in junior high school that launched her burning desire to act, and then later, as Shelley Winters, obtained increasingly important roles on the stage and in movies. Rose's advice to Shelley was given to her as Rose was dying in the intensive-care unit after her third heart attack. After two Oscars, four hit plays, and ninety-six films, Shelley Winters describes her mother as "the source of my strength, talent, chutzpah, and ingenuity, and the lady I clung to no matter how many times I left home or got married."

SOURCE:
Shelley Winters, *Shelley, Also Known as Shirley* (New York: William Morrow and Co., 1980).

FAMOUS CHILD:	Reba McEntire
MOTHER'S NAME:	Jacqueline "Jackie" Smith McEntire
MAMA SAID:	*"Reba, I never got to do this and I always wanted to. So if I push you too hard or if I insist on you doing some things that you don't want to do, it's just because I'm going to live my musical career through you."*

Jackie Smith always loved to sing and some even said she sounded like Patsy Cline. However, her deeply religious parents discouraged a career in entertainment, and their dutiful daughter went to college, became a schoolteacher, married Oklahoma rancher Clark McEntire, and had four children. When she observed that her third child, Reba Nell, born in 1955, had a real love of singing to go with a beautiful voice, Jackie vowed to do what she could to help Reba have a singing career.

Reba recalls in her biography, *Reba*, that her mother taught her kids harmony, often while singing in the car as they traveled to their father's rodeos. It wasn't long before Reba was singing the national anthem at the rodeo. When country singer, songwriter, and music publisher Red Steagall heard her sing at a 1974 rodeo, he invited her to Nashville to try out some of his songs. Reba and her mother made the six-hundred-mile drive from Oklahoma, during which Jackie shared her dream with Reba and after which Reba left with her first recording contract.

Reba recalled the incident in 1987 after winning her fourth Country Music Association Vocalist of the Year Award, stating that her mother was always there to give her the "extra push when I'm tired or I'm homesick." However, Reba also remarked that "she didn't push me until it all fell into place, kinda like she knew it would someday fall into place when I was mature enough to handle it."

After several difficult years marred by a divorce and a tragic airplane crash which killed her entire band in 1991, Reba remarried and, at age thirty-five, became a mother herself. She regularly consults her former schoolteacher mother for advice regarding child-care problems and the many complications that come with mothering within the limits of a very active professional life.

SOURCES:

Don Cusic, *Reba, Queen of Country Music* (New York: St. Martin's Press, 1991).

Candace Bushnell, "What Reba Did for Love," *Good Housekeeping*, July 1995.

elen Keller, born in Tuscumbia, Alabama, in 1880, was the first child of a captain in the Confederate army whose ancestor was the first teacher of the deaf in Zurich, Switzerland, and who had written a book outlining the education of the deaf—"rather a singular coincidence," according to Helen in her 1954 autobiography. Her mother, Kate Keller, was the daughter of a Confederate brigadier-general, born in Massachusetts but relocated to Arkansas.

Ambition

Helen Keller said, "I came, I saw, I conquered, as the first child in a family always does." Early on, she was known for her bright, inquisitive, self-asserting, and eager manner, while she imitated everyone, first spoke at six months of age, and walked at one year. "These happy days didn't last long," she goes on in her autobiography, for at nineteen months, she came down with "acute congestion of the stomach and brain" which "closed my eyes and ears and plunged me into the unconsciousness of a new baby." Helen Keller would never hear or see again.

Kate Adams taught her blind and deaf daughter many things during the next several years, but the family at the same time witnessed Helen's increasingly frequent tantrums, as she found it more and more difficult to communicate. As an adult, Helen noted, "I owe her. My mother succeeded in making me understand a great deal."

Kate Keller dedicated herself to finding an education for her deaf and blind daughter at a time when special education for the physically challenged was scarce. It also seemed unlikely that anyone would come to such a faraway place as Tuscumbia to teach a child both deaf and blind, and many friends and relatives thought that it was doubtful that she could be taught at all. "My mother's only ray of hope came from Charles Dickens's *American Notes*. She read his account of Laura Bridgman, and remembered vaguely that she was deaf and blind, yet had been educated." With an ambition for her daughter, in spite of her profound handicap, Kate Adams sought educational help, which connected her to the Perkins School for the Blind in Massachusetts, and eventually to Anne Sullivan, an 1886 graduate of the school. At the age of six, Helen Keller was introduced to the young woman who eventually moved into the Keller home and succeeded in opening up her world.

Teacher Anne Sullivan received a letter from Laura Bridgman in 1887 which she read to Kate Keller at the supper table. Kate Keller immediately exclaimed, "Why Miss Annie, Helen writes almost as well as that now!" At seven years old, only months after Anne Sullivan's arrival, Helen had already made great progress in her studies. Kate Keller knew then that her ambition and hope for her daughter could eventually translate into reality.

Helen Keller graduated from Radcliffe College in 1904, wrote, lectured, and raised funds for others like her for the rest of her life. The story of teacher and child was chronicled in *The Miracle Worker*, a Pulitzer prize–winning play performed in 1960, and later made into a movie.

SOURCE:
Helen Keller, *Helen Keller: The Story of My Life* (Doubleday and Co., 1954).

FAMOUS CHILD:	**Douglas MacArthur**
MOTHER'S NAME:	**Mary Pinkney "Pinky" MacArthur**
MAMA SAID:	*"You must grow up to be a great man."*

*P*inky MacArthur was the daughter of a Virginia cotton baron and Civil War hero. While he was somewhat dismayed by her planned marriage to Arthur MacArthur, a Union Civil War hero, his strong-willed daughter persisted. A military family, they were assigned to the Fort Selden military base in New Mexico. MacArthur would later say, "My first recollection was that of a bugle call."

Life on a military base was difficult during the ten-year

period they lived there from 1880–1890. His mother turned her attention to her son. She tutored him in the three R's and tried to foster a sense of obligation in him. The future war hero recalled some of her early messages: "Do what is right," "Never lie and tattle," and "Our country comes first." When she put him to bed at night, she would remind him of her expectations, often exhorting him to be a great man like his father or Robert E. Lee. The fact that his father and Lee were on opposite sides of the Civil War conflict mattered less to her than the fact that both had fought well for their cause.

In William Manchester's book about MacArthur, entitled *American Caesar*, he states that Pinky "realized her own ambition through the exploits of her men." When Douglas was accepted to West Point in 1899, she took an apartment in a nearby hotel where she could see that her son was keeping his light on and studying. Later in MacArthur's career, and to his dismay, she went so far as to write letters to her friend, Chief of Staff General Pershing, urging him to give Douglas a promotion to Major General. He was given the promotion ten days before Pershing's term ended.

Manchester goes on to state that MacArthur was a "well-born victim of *Uberangstlichkeit*, (a German phrase for mama's boy) who reached his fullest dimension in following maternal orders to be mercilessly ambitious." MacArthur did just that. Manchester notes that he became the "most gifted man-at-arms this nation has produced," winning twenty-two medals, including thirteen for heroism in the major wars in the first half of the twentieth century.

When his mother died in the Philippines in 1935 at the age of eighty-four, MacArthur subsequently arranged to have her body moved to Washington where she was buried in Arlington National Cemetery.

SOURCE:
William Manchester, *American Caesar* (New York: Dell Publishing, 1978).

Courage

Martin Luther King

Nelson Mandela

Henry Kissinger

Geraldine Ferraro

Jackie Robinson

Chris Burke

Hans Christian Andersen

Andrew Jackson

Carl Sandburg

Sojourner Truth

Courage

🦁 Generations of children have accompanied Dorothy along the yellow brick road as her friend, the Cowardly Lion, in the *Wizard of Oz*, sought courage. His search for the resolution, valor, spirit, and spunk to stand tall in times of danger or difficulty is legendary.

Andrew Jackson, whose own courage was inspired by his mother's actions during the Revolutionary War, later said, "One man with courage makes a majority." A mother's courage forms the foundation for her child's use of it during times of challenge later in life. By exemplifying this virtue, mothers demonstrate courage by word and deed to their children.

It takes courage to overcome bias and discrimination. Several of our celebrity stories involve mothers whose children learned that lesson well. Mallie Robinson moved to California and sacrificed in order to support her large, impoverished family after her husband left. Carrying this banner of courage, her son Jackie Robinson broke baseball's racial barrier many years later and became the first black player in the major leagues. Alberta King listened at the dinner table as young Martin told her that his white friend could not play with him anymore now that they were in school. The proud mother related the history of slavery and discrimination to her son, while impressing upon him that he was just as important as anyone else. This pride and courage remained with Martin Luther King for the rest of his life.

Ma-Ma Betts gave her young daughter, Belle, religious faith to sustain her courage throughout a difficult childhood. Born into slavery in about 1797, Belle was regularly beaten and treated cruelly. Later known as Sojourner Truth, she went on to travel, to teach about God, and to courageously champion human rights among her people.

Several mothers made extreme sacrifices to provide their children with opportunity. Paula Kissinger, of Jewish descent, moved her family out of Germany, at no small risk, to escape Nazi persecution. Three months later when the Kissingers' temple was burned, fifteen-year-old Henry was safely in America, thanks to his mother's courageous exodus.

Similarly, when Nosekeni Fanny's husband died she knew that she was in no position to take care of her young son effectively. She courageously gave him to a local chief to raise. As a grown adult, Nelson Mandela exemplified his mother's courage as he championed the rights of his native South African people.

Sometimes courage is seen in quiet strength. In *Reckless Ecstasy*, a book of poems and prose that Carl Sandburg dedicated to his mother, he characterized his mother as "the one who has kept a serene soul in a life of stress, wrested beauty from the commonplace, and scattered her gladness without stint or measure."

The courage shown by these mothers in this chapter provided a foundation for their children to build upon when they confronted difficult times as adults. Many times this message was unspoken. Other times it was modestly demonstrated. Henrik Ibsen said it best in 1890: "Oh courage . . . oh yes! If only one had that . . . Then life might be livable, in spite of everything."

FAMOUS CHILD:	Martin Luther King, Jr.
MOTHER'S NAME:	Alberta Williams King
MAMA SAID:	*"You must never feel that you are less than anybody else. You must always feel that you are somebody."*

artin Luther King's closest playmate in Atlanta as a preschooler was a white boy whose father owned a store across the street from the King home. In 1935, according to biographer Stephen B. Oates, the two friends entered separate schools, after which the friend's parents announced that Martin Luther could no longer play with their son. "But why?" he sputtered. "Because we are white and you are colored."

It was later during dinner at home that young Martin

related this episode to his parents, and for the first time, according to Oates, they told him about the "race problem." They recounted the history of slavery and issues surrounding the Civil War, the presidency of Abraham Lincoln, and finally the extraordinary abilities that he, young Martin, possessed. It was at the end of this "disturbing and shocking" episode in the education of young Martin Luther King that Alberta King made this courageous statement of support.

Alberta King, a "short, subdued woman, quiet, deliberate, and slow to anger," was the daughter of the pastor of Atlanta's Ebenezer Baptist Church, Reverend Adam Daniel Williams, who had held this position since 1894. After Reverend Adam's death in 1931, Alberta's own husband Martin Luther King, Sr. became pastor of the same church where Alberta played the organ for the choir. Born on January 15, 1929, Martin Luther King, Jr. grew up in the church with his family. Here "M. L. knew who he was—Reverend King's boy, somebody special." According to Oates, M. L. was a "gifted and brilliant child who loved books, learning, had a phenomenal memory, and who could talk like he was grown up sometimes."

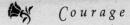

"Wait and see," said young M. L. to his parents. "When I grow up I'm going to get me some big words." The scholarly and eloquent Martin Luther King, Jr. went on to become a spokesperson for nonviolence, racial justice, and equality during a time of great turmoil in America.

SOURCE:
Stephen B. Oates, *Let the Trumpet Sound: A Life of Martin Luther King, Jr.* (New York: HarperCollins, 1994).

FAMOUS CHILD:	Rolihlahla (Nelson) Mandela
MOTHER'S NAME:	Nosekeni Fanny
MAMA SAID:	*"Uqinisufokotho, Kwedini!* *(Brace yourself, my boy!)"*

These were the only words nine-year-old Nelson's mother could find to say when she left him in the care of the local regent following the death of Nelson's father. Mandela noted in his autobiography that his mother's "tender look was all the affection and support I needed."

Mandela's father had been a Xhosa leader who earlier had played a key role in helping the regent become chief. His widowed mother now realized that the regent would be able to provide an advantageous upbringing and education for her bright young son.

Nelson, as he was named when he started school in the British system at age seven, was given the name Rolihlahla at his birth in 1918. This means "pulling the branch of a tree," which Mandela indicated may have been a predictor of the many storms he caused and weathered in his life.

Mandela states that his mother often told him Xhosa stories and fables which had been passed down for generations. He recalled the story of two travelers who met an elderly woman afflicted with unsightly cataracts covering her eyes. The first traveler refused her request for help. When the second one courageously obliged, aiding her with the unpleasant task of cleaning her eyes, the scales mysteriously fell off, and the woman became young and beautiful. The traveler then married her and became young and prosperous. Mandela noted the enduring message from his mother's fable that "virtue and generosity will be rewarded in ways that one cannot know."

He would not see his mother until, as a young man, he was about to be jailed. He saw her again in jail shortly before her death in 1968. Mandela, who championed the anti-apartheid movement in South Africa, spent twenty-six years in jail before being released in 1990. He was given a Nobel prize in 1993 for his efforts in leading the transition to South Africa's first multiracial democracy.

SOURCE:
Nelson Mandela, *Long Walk to Freedom: The Autobiography of Nelson Mandela* (Boston: Little, Brown and Co., 1994).

*I*n the spring of 1938, when Henry was fifteen, Paula Kissinger saw the imminent danger her Jewish family faced should they remain in Germany. Quickly, leaving her own dying parents behind, she moved her family to the United States. She later indicated her fear of Hitler and his extermination of Jews by noting, "In my heart, I knew that they would have burned us with the others if we had stayed." Three months later, the mobs of Kristallnacht destroyed their synagogue and many others, beginning an extended nightmare that would eventually cost thirteen close relatives of the Kissingers' their lives.

Kissinger, who became secretary of state during the Nixon presidential years of the 1970s, is known for his courageous approach to many vexing international issues of the time. He developed the policy of détente to deal peacefully with the Russian military menace of the time, worked carefully between political doves and hawks to extricate the United States from the Vietnam War, and overcame many diplomatic barriers making possible the historic Nixon breakthrough visit to China.

At his mother's ninetieth birthday celebration in 1991, Kissinger told her, "In a time of adversity, you were the one who held us together through your courage and spirit and devotion. Everything I have achieved, that our family has achieved, is due to you." His mother, brimming with pride, responded that "It was worth to have lived a life for."

SOURCE:
Walter Isaacson, *Kissinger: A Biography* (New York: Simon & Schuster, 1992).

FAMOUS CHILD:	**Geraldine Ferraro**
MOTHER'S NAME:	**Antonetta Ferraro**
MAMA SAID:	*"Don't forget your name. 'Ferro' means iron. You can bend it, but you can't break it. Go on."*

*A*fter her husband's death, Antonetta was left at the age of thirty-nine with two young children to raise, one of whom was Geraldine Ferraro, the first woman ever nominated by a major political party for Vice President of the United States. Geraldine kept her mother's name professionally after she married, in tribute to her mother, a woman who never complained and who taught her daughter "by work and example how important it was for men and women to be self-sufficient."

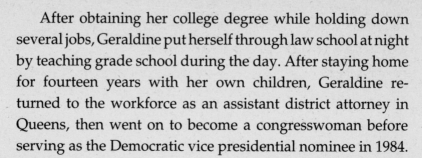

After obtaining her college degree while holding down several jobs, Geraldine put herself through law school at night by teaching grade school during the day. After staying home for fourteen years with her own children, Geraldine returned to the workforce as an assistant district attorney in Queens, then went on to become a congresswoman before serving as the Democratic vice presidential nominee in 1984.

SOURCE:
Geraldine Ferraro with Linda Bird Francke, *Ferraro: My Story* (New York: Bantam Books, 1985).

FAMOUS CHILD:	Jackie Robinson
MOTHER'S NAME:	Mallie Robinson
MAMA DID:	*Demonstrated courage by supporting family through difficult times.*

allie Robinson demonstrated courage when she moved her family from the South to California after her husband had abandoned her and her five young children.

Jackie Robinson is known for his courage as the first black person to play in previously segregated major-league baseball with the Brooklyn Dodgers in 1947. He recalled his mother's own courage years before, when at the time she had a choice of returning to the plantation where the family had worked or moving to an uncertain future in California where her brother lived. Robinson notes in his biography, "even though there appeared to be little future for us in the West, my mother knew that there she could be assured of the basic necessities." He claims that his mother indoctrinated the family with the importance of religion, family unity, and kindness toward others.

He states, "I remember even as a small boy, having a lot of pride in my mother. I thought she must have some kind of magic to be able to do all the things she did, to work hard and never complain and to make us feel happy. . . . At an early age, I began to want to relieve her in any small way I could."

Robinson, after courageously overcoming numerous racial attacks early in his career, had an outstanding major-league career. He led the Dodgers to six World Series appearances in ten years, was named Most Valuable Player in 1949, and was elected to the Baseball Hall of Fame in 1962.

SOURCE:
Alfred Duckett, *Jackie Robinson: I Never Had It Made, an Autobiography as told to . . .* (New York: G. P. Putnam's Sons, 1972).

FAMOUS CHILD:	Chris Burke
MOTHER'S NAME:	Marian Brady Burke
MAMA SAID:	*"We never gave a thought to the doctor's advice. He was mine and I was going to take him home no matter what."*

When Marian Burke's fourth child, Chris, was born with Down's syndrome in 1965 in New York City, the doctor advised Marian and her police-man husband, Frank, to put the infant in an institution and to forget him. "It will be the best thing for you and for your family." Marian, Frank, and Chris's three older siblings, twelve, fourteen, and sixteen, knew that they had a lot to learn, but one thing was perfectly clear: They would raise Chris at home with plenty of love and guidance, and would never hide him or be ashamed of him. Infant Chris Burke had tested positive for trisomy 21, which indicated that he had three instead of the normal two copies of chromosome 21. This is called Down's syndrome (widely labeled mongolism in 1965) and is usually associated with a diminished intellectual capacity.

Marian, born into a strong Irish-American family in the Bronx, continued this close family tradition in her own, and courageously focused her and her family's efforts on remaining positive, teaching little Chris everything he could possibly learn, and taking pride in each and every accomplishment. Celebrating and photographing every milestone and including Chris in all activities, the positive and courageous family watched their son and sibling attain every goal. "He just took a little longer at each phase," Marian added. (It wasn't until the 1980s that educators found that early intervention comprised of stimulating games, exercises, and positive attention could lead to better behavior and increased learning in children with Down's syndrome.)

As Chris grew and matured, he became interested in acting while watching his siblings go all around New York City on acting and modeling jobs. He developed a strong

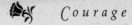

interest in television family sitcoms, often able to recite entire scripts, while telling friends that he'd be on TV someday. After many starring roles in school plays, and with the support of his family, Chris Burke was selected as the lead in the 1980s popular television show, *Life Goes On*, in the role of Corky Thacher.

Chris Burke, supported by his mother, father, and siblings, became a courageous ambassador for those who are handicapped. His extraordinary gift for eloquently expressing the trials of growing up "different" has allowed him to mentor those with disabilities and serve as an example of courage and hope.

SOURCE:
Chris Burke and Jo Beth McDaniel, *A Special Kind of Hero* (New York: Dell Publishing, 1991).

Hans Christian Andersen, born in Odense, Denmark, in 1805, grew into a tall, thin, sensitive, emotional young man inspired by the mythology of his culture and books by Holberg and Voltaire, the Bible, and the *Arabian Nights* read to him by his cobbler father. "Once when he and his mother were toiling with a group of gleaners," according to biographer Monica Stirling, "a bailiff known for his savage temper advanced on them with upraised whip." Everyone fled except for Hans

Christian who was deep in thoughts of the "biblical story of Ruth and Naomi gleaning in the fields of Boaz." Looking straight at the angry bailiff, and mustering a courage older than his years, the child asked, "How can you dare to strike me when God can see you?" To everyone's amazement, "the bailiff patted the boy's cheek, asked his name and gave him some money." Anne Marie, perplexed and used to harsh treatment, made the remark to her neighbors.

Anne Marie, an illiterate washerwoman and illegitimate child raised by her grandmother, was determined that her son, Hans Christian, would see "as little as possible of the sordid aspects of poverty," according to biographer Monica Stirling. She often told young Hans how much luckier he was than she had been. Once a year in May, Anne Marie would take Hans to the woods to welcome spring, which was heralded by the return of the storks. The mythology and superstitions associated with the woods of his native land and early memories of his childhood inspired Hans throughout his life, providing the base from which his later fairy tales emerged. His mother's account of being tossed out by her parents into the street to beg, was the inspiration for Hans Christian Andersen's tale, "The Little Match Girl."

Hans Christian Andersen as an adult had vivid memories of his mother's garden, just a little wooden box planted with chives and parsley. "In the story of 'The Snow Queen' that garden still blooms," he once said.

Hans Christian Andersen courageously left Odense at the age of fourteen for Copenhagen with only a love of theater, desire for recognition, and letters of introduction. Many years later, after a career of storymaking which delighted children of all ages, Hans Christian Andersen said, "First you endure terrible hardship, then you become famous."

SOURCE:
Monica Stirling, *The Wild Swan* (New York: Harcourt, Brace & World, 1965).

FAMOUS CHILD:	Andrew Jackson
MOTHER'S NAME:	Elizabeth "Betty" Hutchinson Jackson
MAMA SAID:	*"In this world you will have to make your own way. To do that, you must have friends. You can make friends by being honest, and you can keep them by being steadfast."*

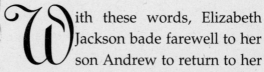

With these words, Elizabeth Jackson bade farewell to her son Andrew to return to her nursing responsibilities during the Revolutionary War. When she became ill and died on her mission, the words became the last ones that fourteen-year-old Andrew would hear from her.

Elizabeth and her husband had emigrated to America in 1765 and struggled to find a homestead in the Carolina wilderness. When her husband died two days before the birth of their third child, Andrew, Betty was forced to raise her family in a harsh time. Although she expressed hope that Andrew might some day become a minister, she saw in her temperamental young son a distinct personality and a need to lead his life in his own way. When the Revolutionary War came to the rural Carolinas, Betty and her children courageously joined the battle. Andrew's two brothers died, as did his mother shortly after. Jackson later recalled, "Her last words have been the law of my life. The memory of my mother and her teachings were the only capital I had to start my life with, and on that capital I have made my way."

Historians have characterized Jackson, known as "Old Hickory," for his courage as a soldier, most notably at the battle of New Orleans in 1814, but also in his political life as orator, statesman, congressman, and the seventh president of the United States. This image is defined in a quote attributed to him: "One man with courage makes a majority." Jackson later in his life credited his mother's spirit as a major influence on his life, remembering her as "gentle as a dove and brave as a lioness."

SOURCES:

Burke Davis, *Old Hickory: A Life of Andrew Jackson* (New York: Dial Press, 1977).

Mabel Bartlett and Sophia Baker, *Mothers, Makers of Men* (Exposition Press, 1952).

FAMOUS CHILD:	Carl August Sandburg
MOTHER'S NAME:	Clara Sandburg
MAMA SAID:	*"You can do the best you can, and maybe you make a name for yourself. It don't do any hurt to try."*

*P*oet, journalist, and biographer of Abraham Lincoln, Carl Sandburg was born in Illinois in 1878, the second child and first son of thrifty, hardworking Swedish immigrants. His father, August, worked fourteen-hour days, six days a week, on the railroad, leaving young Carl, "a consistently good student," in the company of his good-natured mother, a woman with "visions and hopes" and an "eagerness about books."

Born in Appuna, Sweden, young Clara became moth-

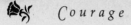

erless at the age of six, leaving home as a teen to work as a hotel maid in Galesburg, Illinois, after hearing glowing reports from relatives who had settled there. Clara raised her children with generous affection, patience, and courage. Biographer Penelope Niven describes Carl Sandburg's poems as "reverberating with images of people who, like August and Clara, bent their lives to the weight of the work they had to do."

The constant of good-natured, calm mothering that Carl Sandburg received during his poor but solid childhood as the son of Swedish immigrants, gave him the courage to weather the storms of life, champion in his poetry the image of the ordinary man, and become a poet of the people. Hard times forced young Carl to go to work in eighth grade, and later he wrestled with depression leading to thoughts of suicide. Very quickly, however, he concluded that "if luck didn't come your way it was up to you to step into the struggle and like it."

His mother's courageous outlook in an often difficult life gave her son a solid base upon which to forge his struggle. This foundation of courage launched Carl's long and successful literary career and his first book, *In Reckless Ecstacy*, a book of poems and prose dedicated to his mother— "the one who has kept a serene soul in a life of stress, wrested beauty from the commonplace, and scattered her gladness without stint or measure."

SOURCE:
Penelope Niven, *Carl Sandburg: A Biography* (New York: Charles Scribner's Sons, 1991).

FAMOUS CHILD:	Sojourner Truth (formerly Isabelle, Belle Hardenbergh, or Colonel Hardenbergh's Belle)
MOTHER'S NAME:	Ma-Ma Betts
MAMA SAID:	*"The Mighty Being is a God who sees you and hears you." Belle asked, "Where does he live?" Ma-Ma Betts answered, "High in the sky. When you are beaten or cruelly treated, or fall into trouble, just ask him for help. He will always hear and help you."*

*a*round 1797, Sojourner Truth was born "Isabelle" to slave parents, Ma-Ma Betts and Bomefree, who were both slaves of Colonel Hardenbergh, a large land owner and farmer in Ulster County, New York, on the Hudson River.

By 1828 New York had freed all slaves and in 1843, at the age of forty-six, Belle left her life as a domestic servant and set out to travel, to preach about God, and to teach against slavery. She took the name Sojourner Truth to symbolize her new life. Sojourner represented "traveler" and Truth "to declare truth unto the people." According to biographer Jacqueline Bernard, Sojourner Truth "championed women's rights, prison reform and better working conditions" for working people after the Civil War, "assisting freedmen of the South as they traveled north, looking for work, land, and freedom."

Sojourner Truth, as a child, benefited from her mother's rich and solid belief system. It would sustain her throughout her difficult life as a slave and as a leader of her people. She found the courage to deal with the tragedy of watching her brothers and sisters sold—never to be seen again—in her mother's exclamation while stargazing one night: "Right this minute, those same stars you see are shining down on all your brothers and sisters. No matter where they are, they see those stars as plain as you."

SOURCE:
Jacqueline Bernard, *Journey Toward Freedom: The Story of Sojourner Truth* *(New York: W. W. Norton & Company, 1967).*

Devotion

Hume Cronyn

Dan Jansen

Elvis Presley

Leonard Bernstein

Emmitt Smith

Dr. Charles Mayo

Jack Benny

Sally Jessy Raphaël

Bill Cosby

Larry King

Sigmund Freud

Bill Russell

Franklin Delano Roosevelt

Roger Clemens

Van Cliburn

Duke Ellington

Judy Garland

Devotion

Look behind a successful person and you will often find a devoted mother. This mother provided affection, dedication, and loyalty for her child to use in his/her quest for success. She planted a seed of self-esteem in her child which took root, started to grow, and became the groundwork upon which to build a life. Children who grow up with this virtue know they are cherished.

Devoted mothers create a climate of affection that fosters their child's ability to grow and succeed. The devotion between Gladys Presley and her son Elvis is legendary. It inspired him to dedicate his first record, "That's All Right, Mama," to her. Likewise, basketball legend Bill Russell benefited from a devoted mother. He wrote, "Everybody knew

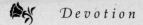

that Katie Russell was sweet on me and that she stood by me like a fierce guardian."

A devoted mother knows her child's strengths and is dedicated to his/her development. Though Emma Kubelsky watched her son stumble through his school years daydreaming, playing truant, and receiving bad grades, she refused to give up on him. Recognizing that he had a talent for playing the violin, Emma attended concerts, supported his efforts, and lived to see her son, comedian Jack Benny, entertain audiences everywhere. Sally Jessy Raphaël's mother Dede recognized that her teenaged daughter wasn't always pleased with her grades and appearance. Rather than focus on her daughter's difficulties, Dede chose to focus on her strengths while bolstering Sally Jessy's confidence. "Does anyone else in your class know how to recite Shakespeare the way you do?" she said.

A mother's devotion to her family or to a family cause models this virtue for her child. For example, Jerry Jansen made it clear that she valued not only her son Dan but the family as a whole. Gerry's philosophy was simple: If one Jansen goes somewhere, they all go. The entire family supported Dan's quest for a gold medal and sustained each other during the terminal illness of their daughter and sister.

The Mayo Clinic in Rochester, Minnesota, is a model of family devotion. Founded in 1863 by Dr. William Mayo, the clinic has had a Mayo on staff most every year since. Edith Mayo, a Mayo clinic nurse and devoted supporter, advised her future daughter-in-law, "Remember, the Clinic will always come first, then you, then your children."
Shakespeare said in *Hamlet*,

> 'Tis too much, prov'd—that with devotion's visage
> And pious action, we do sugar o'er
> The devil itself.

A child who grows up with devotion is well on a road to success. The following stories illustrate this timeless message.

FAMOUS CHILD:	Hume Cronyn
MOTHER'S NAME:	Frances Labatt Cronyn
MAMA SAID:	*"You must not be angry with them. They are only thinking of your own good. I will make a bargain with you—go back to the university for one more year, and if at the end of that time you still wish to go into the theatre, I will see to it that you go to the Royal Academy in London, or to the American Academy in New York—as you choose."*

Hume Cronyn grew up in London, Ontario, in a prominent, wealthy, extended family of loving and strong characters in a mansion named "Woodfield" built by his great-grandfather, an Irish cleric from Dublin. Hume, the unconventional fifth child, drove a Franklin Roadster in a raccoon coat and said he "even brought an actor—a real live professional actor— home with him for the week-end," initiating comments from more conventional members of the family about his being overindulged and spoiled.

Frances Cronyn, under pressure from more conventional family members, well aware that young Hume wasn't pleased with the course of study he was pursuing at McGill, but still devoted and supportive of her son, came up with this compromise. Her devotion and support, extended at the time of such family pressure, allowed young Hume to finish out the year at McGill while continuing to dream of a career in the acting profession. Soon after he left for New York City in the midst of the Depression to follow his muse. It wasn't long before Hume and his new wife, actress Jessica Tandy, were headed for Hollywood where they both succeeded in building a marriage and acting careers, each of which spanned more than fifty years.

SOURCE:
Hume Cronyn, *A Terrible Liar: A Memoir*, (New York: William Morrow and Co., 1991).

The Olympic gold-medal winner noted in his autobiography that while mom's rule probably cost him a few overnight visits with friends, it did promote a sense of closeness and devotion among his family. Jansen concluded that "if we can all give our kids what our parents gave us, we all will have been successful parents." Dan's family (including his sister Jane, who died of cancer in 1988) was there in either body or spirit as he won a gold medal at the 1992 Lillehammer Olympics.

SOURCE:
Dan Jansen with Jack McCallum, *Full Circle: An Olympic Champion Shares His Breakthrough Story* (New York: Villard Books, 1994).

FAMOUS CHILD:	Elvis Presley
MOTHER'S NAME:	Gladys Love Smith Presley
MAMA SAID:	*"Son, take this guitar—you're not going to get a rifle. Take it and play it."*

Elvis's mother exposed him at age two to music through her church choir. He later said he knew then that he had to sing. Despite a family life made difficult by limited finances, Gladys showed her devotion to young Elvis by teaching him to be respectful, hard-working, and loving.

She bought him his first guitar at age nine. He would make good use of the gift. In fact, his first record was a tribute to his mom. Sam Phillips of Sun Records, who signed Elvis Presley to his first contract, said that "it all started because a kid wanted to make a record for his mom." Elvis had always been close to Gladys—so close that he took her instructions to heart. Always seeking to please her, he titled his first recording "That's All Right, Mama."

At her 1958 funeral he cried and said, "I love you so much. I lived my whole life for you. Oh, God, everything I have is gone."

SOURCES:

"Elvis Presley," on *Biography* on the Arts and Entertainment Network, February 8, 1995.

Larry Geller and Joel Spector with Patricia Romanowski, *If I Can Dream: Elvis' Own Story* (New York: Avon Books, 1989).

FAMOUS CHILD:	Leonard Bernstein
MOTHER'S NAME:	Jennie Bernstein
MAMA SAID:	*"Lenny always wanted an audience. And in the beginning, I was his audience."*

*J*ennie Bernstein told author Meryle Secrest that one of her motherly roles was to serve as young Lenny's chief listener. He could always keep her listening to him play late into the night by flattering her and asking her which ending of a piece she liked best.

Bernstein, who grew up outside Boston, started piano lessons at age ten. He quickly progressed, noting that he soon played the Chopin E-flat Nocturne with such intensity that his mother would cry. She continued to encourage her son's playing, often to the dismay of their complaining neighbors to whom she would respond, "Some day you're going to pay to hear him." Of course, Leonard would not lack for audiences in his long career as a composer, pianist, and conductor until his death at age seventy-two in 1990.

Humphrey Burton, in his biography of Bernstein, points out that for Jennie's eighty-eighth birthday in 1986, Bernstein included in his autobiographical suite a song with a slow waltz tempo entitled "First Love (for my Mother, March 1986)." The lyric revolved around the numerical coincidence between his mother's age and the eighty-eight keys on the piano, his own first love.

SOURCES:

Meryle Secrest, *Leonard Bernstein: A Life* (New York: Alfred A. Knopf, 1994).

Humphrey Burton, *Leonard Bernstein* (New York: Doubleday and Co., 1994).

FAMOUS CHILD:	Emmitt Smith
MOTHER'S NAME:	Mary Smith
MAMA SAID:	*"Yes, they talk about his speed. Well, they never saw what he was capable of. They never saw all the 90-yard runs of his in peewee league. I never did see anyone catch him from behind once he had a ball under his arms."*

We don't need mom to tell us, as she did in *Sports Illustrated* prior to the 1990 NFL draft, about Super Bowl MVP Emmitt Smith's breakaway speed. There is something far more telling in the fact that she was there to see him so frequently in the first place. Mary Smith's steadfast devotion to her superstar-to-be made possible his tremendous success. He noted in his autobiography that "it was always 'Mom, Mom, Mom'" who signed him up for youth football and encouraged him to pursue his considerable talents.

SOURCE:
Emmitt Smith with Steve Delsohn, *The Emmitt Zone* (New York: Crown Publishers, 1994).

FAMOUS CHILD:	Dr. Charles Mayo
MOTHER'S NAME:	Edith Graham Mayo
MAMA SAID:	*"A doctor's calling is a sacred calling and only high-minded men should enter the ranks. It is our earnest prayer that you and Joseph may meet this requirement."*

When Charles Mayo first entered medical school, he was given this advice by his mother, Edith Graham Mayo, the first trained nurse in Rochester, Minnesota. She already for many years had devotedly supported her husband in his career and had given her own efforts as a nurse to the Mayo Clinic legacy in Rochester, which had begun in 1863 when the founder Dr. William Worrall Mayo hung out his shingle.

Edith gave this timely advice to her future daughter-in-law, Alice, before her marriage to Dr. Charles Mayo: "You're going to do just what I did, exactly. You'll find you haven't married a Mayo, you've married the Mayo Clinic. Remember, the Clinic will always come first, then you, then your children." Dr. Mayo added that, "I think Alice discovered that Edith hadn't been exaggerating." It has taken many devoted generations of Mayos to carry on the legacy begun by Dr. William Worrall Mayo in 1863.

SOURCE:
Dr. Charles Mayo, *Mayo: The Story of My Family and My Career* (New York: Doubleday and Co., 1968).

FAMOUS CHILD:	Jack Benny (Benjamin Kubelsky)
MOTHER'S NAME:	Emma Sachs Kubelsky
MAMA SAID:	*"All our sacrifices have been worthwhile. Maybe he isn't such a scholar . . . but he makes beautiful music!"*

On his twelfth birthday, according to his wife Mary, Jack "got a sister and a violin." Jack's immigrant parents felt that if he studied hard, he could become a great symphony violinist, and then "your mother and I will be able to repay our debt to America." However, Jack disliked school. He daydreamed, cut up, played truant, and eventually was expelled, but at the same time he became an outstanding member of his high-school orchestra, playing first violin.

Emma Kubelsky, having experienced years of Jack's school difficulties, was still able to value and focus on what her son did so well. It was at the end of this academic difficulty that his devoted mother Emma, after hearing Jack's solo from "Il Trovatore," whispered this message of pride to her husband.

In 1912, Jack hit the vaudeville circuit with Cora Salisbury as "Salisbury and Kubelsky," playing piano and violin respectively. Doing everything from grand opera to ragtime, Jack soon realized that his comic talent (born of all those years of high-school hijinks) thrilled his audiences. Soon his violin playing took "second fiddle" to his comic routines, and young Jack was on his way to becoming one of the most famous comedians in entertainment history, bolstered by the devotion of a mother who wouldn't give up on her son.

SOURCE:
Mary Livingstone Benny and Hilliard Marks with Marcia Borie, *Jack Benny: A Biography* (New York: Doubleday and Co., 1978).

FAMOUS CHILD:	Sally Jessy Raphaël
MOTHER'S NAME:	Dede Raphaël
MAMA SAID:	*"Does anyone else in your class know how to recite Shakespeare the way you do?"*

S ally Jessy Raphaël spent her childhood fascinated with radio. A great fan of 1950s national radio host Arthur Godfrey, she listened to radio, studied its history, and slowly came upon the notion that radio might hold a career for her. With her father away from their Scarsdale, New York, home on business so much of the time, her mother, Dede, was the "center of my world." Sally says "my mother bolstered my confidence at every turn—and was a stage mother in every sense of the word.

Without stage mothers, you wouldn't have anybody in classical music, ballet, or show business. Somebody has to tell a child that he's got something special."

Dede's support of Sally—she never hesitated to tell her daughter what was special about her—represented the family philosophy that parents should never upbraid a child for his or her weaknesses, in this case less than perfect grades in school. Instead one must encourage a child's strengths. "They zeroed in on what it was that made me feel special about myself and then let me run with it." Sally Jessy Raphaël certainly did run with it, becoming an Emmy award winner with syndicated television and radio shows heard by millions.

SOURCE:
Sally Jessy Raphaël with Pam Proctor, *Sally: Unconventional Success* (New York: William Morrow and Co., 1990).

FAMOUS CHILD: William Henry "Bill" Cosby, Jr.

MOTHER'S NAME: Anna Cosby

MAMA SAID: *"The only thing I had to give him was plenty of love, and oh, dear God, I gave him all I had. But success comes from within, and Bill was determined to be something."*

Bill Cosby was born in 1937 in the Germantown section of North Philadelphia—"the jungle"—in a crowded apartment. Bill's father was a welder and his mother worked fourteen-hour days as a cleaning lady. As the family got larger and the pressures greater, Bill's dad became less and less involved with the family, eventually leaving his mother to raise the family alone. Once Bill became the man of the house, he picked up jobs shining shoes and later bagging groceries to make ends meet. Although Bill dropped out of high school, he kept out of trouble because "if I do so-and-so and get caught and they lock me up, who'll look out for Mom?"

Anna Cosby, devoted to her children, still had time to share "an hour or two reading funny stories about mischievous boys living down in Missouri" after long days at work, according to Bill. He describes these stories by Mark Twain as "the foundation for his humor," which he also attributes to the "unfailing spirits of his mother." When asked by interviewers about his comic influences, Bill would simply say, "Read Twain."

Bill Cosby entertains millions over the world in person, on recordings, and on television as a comic, humorist, and storyteller. He graduated from the University of Massachusetts in Amherst with a Ph.D. in education, and created and starred in his award-winning series *The Cosby Show*.

SOURCE:
Ronald L. Smith, *Cosby* (New York: St. Martin's Press, 1986).

FAMOUS CHILD:	Larry King (Lawrence Harvey Zeiger)
MOTHER'S NAME:	Jennie Gitlitz Zeiger
MAMA SAID:	*"The boy doesn't have a father; he has to help me after school."*

*I*n 1920, Larry's parents emigrated from Russia through Ellis Island to Brooklyn. King wrote of his neighborhood, noting that it possessed "century-old traits from the old country that bonded Jews and Italians into a respect for family values that we felt all around us." With Larry's brother, Irwin, dead of a ruptured appendix by the age of ten, Larry, the oldest, was "pampered, spoiled, and worried over" by his mother. Widowed at forty-three, the devoted mother put her children first, a philosophy that was "always pervasive."

From grade school, when his father died, through high school, Larry remembered that his "motivation had gone south" and unless he liked a subject, he did poorly, relying on "the sympathy of teachers to struggle through—and it worked." With additional sympathy elicited from Larry's teachers by his mother's comment about her "fatherless son," he managed to escape punishment for not doing his homework. Although in the long run this philosophy may have hurt Larry's ability to achieve, in the short run it allowed him the relief from pressure that he was feeling after the death of his father, providing him with a "safety net" and keeping him moving through the system. The devotion demonstrated by Jennie Zeiger was significant, and at a time when she had experienced loss as well.

Larry did succeed many years later as a radio host and host of CNN's *Larry King Live*, bolstered by the devotion of his mother at a difficult time so many years earlier.

SOURCE:
Larry King with Marty Appel, *When You're from Brooklyn, Everything Else Is Tokyo* (Boston: Little, Brown and Co., 1992).

FAMOUS CHILD:	Sigmund Freud
MOTHER'S NAME:	Amalia Nathansohn Freud
MAMA SAID:	*"Sigmund was my golden son."*

Sigmund Freud's mother, Amalia, visibly and audibly worshipped her firstborn son. At age twenty she had become the third wife of Sigmund's father, who was twice her age and who already had children older than she was. The "lively, temperamental, impatient, self-willed, sharp-witted and highly intelligent" Amalia (her grandson's later words) doted on young Sigmund. According to Freud's biographer Peter Gay, this "equipped him for a life of intrepid investigation, elusive fame and halting success."

Gay states that, "Throughout his life as an analyst, Freud recognized the importance of the mother for a child's development." Freud himself wrote, "Above all, a man looks for the memory picture of his mother as it had dominated him since the beginning of his childhood." The importance of this to Freud is illustrated in a 1921 self-analysis when Freud revealed in Latin to his analyst the lingering conflicts in his conscience of seeing his beloved and attractive mother without clothes when he was only two years old.

The famous psychoanalyst, described by W. H. Auden as "no more a person now but a whole climate of opinion," later wrote, "The young man who has been his mother's unquestioned favorite will develop a sense of triumphant self-esteem and, with that, the strength for success in later life."

SOURCE:
Peter Gay, *Freud: A Life for Our Time* (New York: W. W. Norton, 1988).

The mother of basketball legend Bill Russell died at age thirty-two, when he was twelve. The outspoken and somewhat temperamental Russell, who led the Boston Celtics to numerous championships, recalled in his memoirs that she often told him that he was her favorite and she didn't care who knew it. He wrote, "Everybody knew that Katie Russell was sweet on me and that she stood by me like a fierce guardian."

He recalls an incident three years before her death when,

shortly after moving to West Oakland, some bigger kids had wanted to teach the newcomer a lesson and started slapping him around. Seeing this, his mother chased the older boys and made them come back and fight young Bill fairly in front of her. He notes that when the fights were over, "the scrapes and bruises were nothing compared to my mother's proud approval." The pride and devotion demonstrated to him at this early point helped provide Russell with the confidence to face many challenges, both on and off the basketball court.

To understand the roots of this devotion, Russell notes that when he was only two, he suffered a mysterious illness and was taken to a hospital where initial diagnoses failed to disclose the problem. A nearby nun promised to go off and pray. Returning shortly, she took young Bill by the feet and held him upside down until he coughed up a piece of cornbread that had lodged in his throat. He concludes that this incident created a special bond with his mother who would tell the story over and over to illustrate that "I carried a special blessing. I was marked, she believed, and destined for something special and precious."

SOURCE:
Bill Russell and Taylor Branch, *Second Wind: The Memoirs of an Opinionated Man* (New York: Random House, 1979).

FAMOUS CHILD:	Franklin Delano Roosevelt
MOTHER'S NAME:	Sara Delano Roosevelt
MAMA SAID:	*"A mother's eye can always see inwardly the size of a child's foot and everything about him."*

When young Franklin was at private school at Groton in 1897, Sara sent him a pair of shoes with this note. Sara Delano Roosevelt, according to biographer Ted Morgan, was "overwhelming in her devotion; she proclaimed her absolute knowledge and understanding of her son." He adds, "Being an only child gave Franklin a strong core of self-esteem and self-worth, the essential childhood traits that are the foundation of all others."

Franklin Roosevelt, survivor of the crippling disease of polio, leader, governor, and later president of the United States, "dominated American life and did more than any other person in the twentieth century to shape the destiny and course of this nation," according to Morgan. Throughout his life he sustained a close relationship with his mother, who maintained a "position of supremacy in the Roosevelt family."

SOURCE:
Ted Morgan, *FDR: A Biography* (New York: Simon & Schuster, 1985).

FAMOUS CHILD:	**Roger Clemens**
MOTHER'S NAME:	**Bess Wright**
MAMA SAID:	*"I remember watching him pitch in Little League when he was nine. He struck out the side on nine pitches and the catcher's glove made a popping noise. That's when I thought we had something special in the family."*

C y Young Award–winner Roger Clemens, whose parents separated when he was only three months old and whose stepfather died when he was just nine, credits his mother as the "stabilizing force for all my life."

He noted that when he was young, his mother would ride him to baseball practice on the back of her Honda motorcycle. When his talent started to attract the interest of the pros, his devoted mother was there to reject a piddling minor-league contract offered to him after high school. She told the scout, "He already knows how to ride buses." Understanding the importance of her son's education, she convinced him to attend junior college and then the University of Texas.

In his autobiography Clemens showed a full appreciation for the connection between devotion and personal achievement. "In my home and in the programs I played in, I was taught to believe that how I live my life has a bearing on success."

After college he signed with the Boston Red Sox, and became one of the dominant pitchers in the major leagues.

SOURCE:
Roger Clemens with Peter Gammons, *Rocket Man: The Roger Clemens Story* (New York: Penguin Books, 1988).

FAMOUS CHILD:	Harvey Lavan "Van" Cliburn, Jr.
MOTHER'S NAME:	Rildia Bee O'Bryan Cliburn
MAMA SAID:	*"You're not going to play by ear. You're going to really know what you are doing."*

*R*ildia Bee, a child of a socially prominent Texas family, was an accomplished pianist. While her parents did allow her to attend music school in New York, they did not feel it was proper for a young woman to be a performer. Putting aside her music career, Rildia Bee O'Bryan married Lavan Cliburn and soon had a family of her own. She continued to play the piano and give private lessons.

When she heard her three-year-old son Van play by ear the lesson she had just given to one of her music students, she made the above comment. She quickly took her young son under her wing. She became his piano teacher and sat down at the piano with him every day until he was seventeen, telling him at the start, "Now just forget I'm your mother. I'm your piano teacher and we must be serious."

Her son thrived, giving his first recital at four, playing at Carnegie Hall at fourteen, and winning the first Tchaikovsky Piano Competition at twenty-four in Russia in 1958. When asked by a Russian reporter about his mother, Cliburn stated, "She teaches piano."

The win, at the height of the U.S./U.S.S.R. cold war, was Van Cliburn's springboard to an international career that later included concerts for Russian and American leaders. For Russians in 1958, pianist Alexander Toradze noted, "It was the first democratic moment for the Russian people."

Biographer Howard Reich states that Rildia Bee was "at the center of Van's music, his first teacher and predominant influence." Acknowledging this, Cliburn recently recalled that one of his mother's early instructions was, "You must always make it look easy, whether it is or not. Don't make it look like a hazardous health problem."

SOURCE:
Howard Reich, *Van Cliburn* (Nashville: Thomas Nelson, Publishers, 1993).

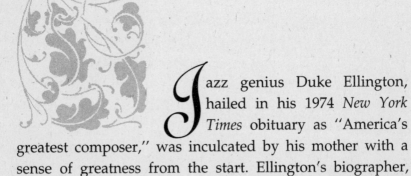

*J*azz genius Duke Ellington, hailed in his 1974 *New York Times* obituary as "America's greatest composer," was inculcated by his mother with a sense of greatness from the start. Ellington's biographer, James Collier, states that, "His boyhood was characterized more than anything by his being a well-loved member of a large, extended family and, especially, by the extraordinary attention paid to him by his mother."

Daisy grew up in a very puritanical, but socially prominent black family in Victorian Washington. She often played the piano, usually semiclassical pieces. She started Duke on piano lessons around age eight to foster his cultural development. Her devotion to her only son certainly made Ellington feel he was special. As Collier notes, "He came to feel that he was, in the precise sense of the word, a little prince." Ellington would make his cousins stand at attention while announcing that he would be "the greatest, the grandest, the glorious Duke."

The closeness between mother and son continued throughout Ellington's life. He chose to live with her for much of his life, buying her expensive gifts and clothing. His son Mercer observed, "His world was built around his mother." When she died in 1935, Ellington was devastated, weeping for days and further expressing his grief with a lavish funeral.

SOURCE:
James Lincoln Collier, *Duke Ellington* (New York: Oxford University Press, 1987).

*J*udy Garland was born in 1922 in Grand Rapids, Minnesota, the third daughter of Frank and Ethel Gumm, who owned the New Grand Theater in the center of town. Judy's older sisters, seven and nine years old, were already performing, singing and dancing, regularly between films or on amateur nights with their parents, who sang and played the ukulele or piano. Ethel Gumm, a plump, spirited five-foot-tall woman with snapping black eyes, rose early each day to cook, bake, sew costumes for the girls, write songs for their performances, play the piano for movies, and in general, manage both the busy household and theater with the assistance of her husband, Frank.

The oldest Gumm sisters doted on their young sister, Baby, a name Judy Garland answered to until the age of twelve. In turn, Baby did her best to mimic their performances and line up behind the girls and their mother on stage, often getting scolded for doing so, leading to her pleas to be included in the act. "Baby, you're too little," Ethel Gumm responded, only to hear young Judy's yells and screams as she pleaded her case. Judy soon won her right to view the acts from behind the stage curtain.

One day Judy and a little friend were taught "My Country Tis of Thee"; her friend faltered, and Judy Garland, at the age of two, in 1925, finished the song with a voice so strong and true, it belied her years. Ethel now found herself repeating to her daughter, "Get off, Baby, you're through," more than once before Frank had to walk out on the stage, throw his daughter over his shoulder, and carry her, still singing, into the wings. A star was born.

Years later, after Judy Garland won an Academy Award for singing "Over The Rainbow" in *The Wizard of Oz*, she began a second career as a concert singer. Judy, demonstrating a magnetism that attracted an international audience, exhibited a devotion to her fans that she had learned from her mother, a woman devoted to her three talented daughters, many years before. Judy Garland, at the height of her successful singing career, said "For such a mixed-up life later, it started out beautifully." Judy's own daughter, Liza Minnelli, has gone on to entertain her own international audiences with much of her mother's and grandmother's energy and style.

SOURCE:
Gerold Frank, *Judy* (New York: Harper & Row, 1975).

Faith

Sting

Muhammad Ali

Loretta Lynn

Mahatma Gandhi

Dolly Parton

Mother Teresa

Robert Frost

Robert Louis Stevenson

Marian Anderson

Naomi Judd

Kathie Lee Gifford

Danny Thomas

Diana Ross

Johnny Cash

Faith

Faith is rooted in a personal belief system and is often, but not always, affiliated with religious beliefs. Whether a mother has introduced her child to belief in a God, or to the inspiration and beauty of nature, she has given him/her a source of lifelong faith. Emily Dickinson's poem, "I Never Saw a Moor," describes the essence of this faith:

> I never saw a moor
> I never saw the sea;
> Yet I know how the heather looks
> And what a wave must be.

I never spoke with God,
nor visited in heaven;
Yet certain am I of the spot
As if the chart were given.

This chapter features a number of mothers whose faith, both religious and secular, was a major source of inspiration to their successful children.

Faith is easiest understood in terms of a religious foundation. Country singers Loretta Lynn and Dolly Parton were inspired by their mothers' religious faith. Loretta Lynn learned to have faith in herself as she overcame marital problems and public inattention to her music before achieving success. Dolly Parton received a quilted patchwork jacket lovingly made by her mother, who fashioned the jacket after Joseph's coat of many colors in the Bible. This coat later became the subject for Dolly's hit recording, "The Coat of Many Colors," a tribute to her mother's faith.

A more secular faith is central to the stories of Sting and Robert Frost. Young Gordon Sumner's faith was given root while listening to his mother play the piano, during which time he was "transported to another world." Faith, together with inborn drive and talent, allowed him to become the international rock star Sting. Likewise, young Robert Frost, influenced by his mother, a poetess herself, found inspiration in nature through the poetry of Emerson and Wordsworth. Robert Frost spent his own lifetime immersed in the creation of poetry celebrating nature's beauty.

The faith demonstrated by Mother Teresa combines both elements. Drana Bojaxhiu's door was "always open to those needing food, shelter, or care." She passed along to her daughter a love for humanity that is central to Mother Teresa's work today. This, combined with a strong Catholic faith, makes Mother Teresa an international icon of faith.

These mothers gave their children faith of many different kinds in many different ways. In each case, however, this virtue provided greater comfort or greater joy, and served as the root of later success. A Biblical passage from Corinthians binds them together: "We walk by faith, not by sight." That faith is often developed and inspired at a mother's knee.

"For my mother," the rock star said, "playing the piano was the only time that I wasn't the center of her world—the only time she ignored me. So I knew that something significant—some important ritual—was being enacted here. I suppose I was being initiated into some sort of mystery. The mystery of music." Despite his platinum-selling success, Sting had one complaint about his genes: "Mother cursed me with the fine ear of a musician but the hands of a plumber."

Sting formed the group Police in 1977 and had many hits in the early 1980s. Since the band broke up in 1986, Sting has become a star in his own name with numerous hit records.

SOURCE:
Commencement address at the Berklee College of Music, Boston, May 15, 1994.

FAMOUS CHILD:	**Muhammad Ali (formerly Cassius Clay)**
MOTHER'S NAME:	**Odessa Clay**
MAMA SAID:	*"I always felt like God made Muhammad special but I don't know why God chose me to carry this child. He had confidence in himself and that gave me confidence in him. The important thing was that he had a belief in God."*

The former heavyweight boxing champion of the world wrote in his biography that his devoted Baptist mother taught him all she knew about God. He notes she took him and his brother to church each Sunday and "taught us the way she thought was right. She taught us to love people and treat everybody with kindness. She taught us it was wrong to be prejudiced or hate."

These quotes illustrate a faith that provided a foundation for Ali's principled life. "I've changed my religion and some of my beliefs since then," Ali wrote, "but her God is still God; I just call him by a different name." Ali will be remembered, not only for his boxing achievements but also for embracing a new religion and standing tall when his boxing title was revoked for his refusal to serve in the Vietnam War.

SOURCE:
Thomas Hauser with the cooperation of Muhammad Ali, *Muhammad Ali: His Life and Times* (New York: Simon & Schuster, 1991).

FAMOUS CHILD:	**Loretta Lynn**
MOTHER'S NAME:	**Clare Marie Webb**
MAMA SAID:	*"If you put four-leaf clovers in a Bible on a page where it says, it will come to pass, it will come to pass."*

hile country-music legend Loretta Lynn might be known as the "coal miner's daughter," it was her American Indian mother whose Bible readings gave her the faith to go on during difficult years. Named after actress Loretta Young, whose photo covered a hole in the wall of the family's eastern Kentucky mountain shack, Loretta married Doolittle Lynn at fourteen. He bought her first guitar, but Loretta credits her mother with teaching her to sing, noting that the first instrument she learned to play was the handsaw as the family gathered at night to sing songs about their lives.

Her mother's role is also seen in a line from the song "Coal Miner's Daughter," describing her mother rocking her babies while reading the Bible at night and getting all the chores done by morning. When her mother died in 1982, a friend observed Loretta could only sit at home and sing, "If I could only hear my mother pray again."

SOURCE:
"Loretta Lynn: Coal Miner's Daughter," on *Biography* on the Arts and Entertainment Network, hosted by Peter Graves, June 21, 1995.

Mahatma Gandhi was born in 1869 in Porbandar along the Arabian Sea, the fourth and last child of his father's fourth and last marriage. Gandhi remembered his mother's saintliness and deeply religious nature, noting that she never "ate a meal without a prayer and attended temple services daily."

During one annual Chaturmas, a kind of Lent lasting through the four-month rainy season, she vowed not to eat unless the sun appeared. Young Gandhi and his siblings would rush in to let their mother know when the sun appeared, only to have it disappear when she followed them outdoors, relates biographer Louis Fischer. "That does not matter," she would comfort her children, "God does not want me to eat today."

This foundation of steadfast purpose, worship, and abstinence modeled by his mother helped Mahatma Gandhi become a great moral leader of the century, prompting the then U.S. secretary of state General George Marshall to call him, upon his death in 1948, "a spokesman for the conscience of all mankind."

SOURCE:
Louis Fischer, *The Life of Mahatma Gandhi* (New York: Harper and Row, 1950).

126

FAMOUS CHILD:	Dolly Parton
MOTHER'S NAME:	Avie Lee Parton
MAMA SANG:	*''Farther along we'll know all about it*
	Farther along we'll understand why
	Cheer up my brother, live in the sunshine
	We'll understand it all by and by.''

*D*olly recalled that her early faith was inspired by Bible stories and old-time mountain songs, like this one sung by her mother to her and her eleven siblings as they sat around the fireplace in their sharecropper cottage in rural Sevier County, Tennessee. As she sang, her mother often quilted by the light of a kerosene lamp, using scraps of material that neighbors often gave Avie Lee because the family was, as Dolly put it, ''poor as Job's turkey.''

Quilting took on increased significance for Dolly as she watched her mother make her a patchwork coat of many colors. It symbolized both her colorful young personality and the Biblical story of Joseph in which a coat of many colors was made to symbolize a child who was loved and special. Dolly recalls the pride she felt as her mother assembled the coat, knowing she was doing this just for her.

The coat, like other aspects of her Smoky Mountain upbringing, eventually became the basis for a hit song entitled "The Coat of Many Colors." It was included on several of Dolly Parton's sixty-two albums which have sold over 50 million copies in what is truly a rags-to-riches story. Dolly calls the song her favorite and noted that after it became a hit she offered to buy her mother a mink coat, only to be rebuffed by Mother who exclaimed, "Shoot! Where would I wear a mink coat, to a pie supper?"

SOURCE:
Dolly Parton, *Dolly, My Life and Other Unfinished Business* (New York: HarperCollins, 1994).

FAMOUS CHILD:	**Mother Teresa (born Ganxhe Agnes Bojaxhiu)**
MOTHER'S NAME:	**Drana Bojaxhiu**
MAMA SAID:	*"When you do good, do it unobtrusively, as if you are tossing a pebble into the sea."*

other Teresa was born in 1910 to Albanian parents to Skopje, Serbia. Her father was a committed Christian so priests and dignitaries were frequent visitors to their home. The family distributed food and money to many people and "their door was always open to those needing food, shelter, or care," according to biographer David Porter. One day Agnes asked, "Who are these people who are guests at our house every day?" Her mother Drana responded, "Some are relatives, but all of them are our people."

Biographer David Porter states that Drana was an "indomitable woman of great strength of character, generous and hardworking. Her home had always been known for its parties and hospitality. Later, after the family had come upon hard times, her home was still famous for the important things: kindness, gentleness, generosity, and compassion toward the poor."

Today, Mother Teresa, displaying an undying faith in humanity, continues to disclaim personal rewards for her lifetime of work. She did, however, accept the Nobel Peace Prize in 1979 for her work as a teacher at the Loreto school in Calcutta and as a founder of her own order, the Missionaries of Charity, which is built on the foundation laid by her mother Drana in Serbia many years before.

SOURCE:
David Porter, *Mother Teresa—The Early Years* (Grand Rapids: William B. Eerdmans Publishing Co., 1986).

FAMOUS CHILD:	Robert Frost
MOTHER'S NAME:	Isabelle Moodie Frost
MAMA SAID:	*"My heart leaps up when I behold a rainbow in the sky."*

Robert Frost, born in San Francisco in 1874, moved to Massachusetts as a child, attended schools there, and spent his career writing poetry that described his much-loved rural New England home. According to biographer Lawrence Thompson, Robert's mother, a poetess herself, made her children feel that romantic nature poetry was at its best when it suggested correspondences between the seen and unseen worlds. Isabelle Frost's quote is from a nineteenth-century Wordsworth poem that she often read to young Robert. It conveyed one of the lessons she learned from poets such as Wordsworth and Emerson, whose works fostered her son's ability to find faith and inspiration in nature. Frost recalled later that Emerson was his favorite poet, probably inspired by an early motherly introduction.

Isabelle believed she had inherited a power of "second sight" from her Scottish grandparents that enabled her to commune with spirits. When young Robert told her that he was hearing voices from his dreams, she confided her own inherited mystical powers of "second sight and hearing," but warned him not to tell others who might misunderstand.

Shortly after her death in 1938, Frost wrote the poem "The Lovely Shall Be Chosen," which he later said was written in commemoration of his mother's difficult life, and which reminds all children never to forget their own mothers' faith and hope.

Robert Frost, whose early ambition was to write "a few poems it will be hard to get rid of," wrote many volumes of poetry. Included in these were well-known poems such as "The Road Not Taken" and the oft-quoted "Stopping By

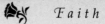

Woods on a Snowy Evening," which lyrically link pastoral images with philosophical thought. Frost is widely regarded as one of the leading poets of the twentieth century and received four Pulitzer prizes for his efforts.

SOURCE:
Lawrence Thompson, *Robert Frost, The Early Years 1874–1915* (New York: Holt, Rinehart and Winston, 1966).

FAMOUS CHILD:	Robert Louis Stevenson
MOTHER'S NAME:	Margaret Balfour Stevenson
MAMA SAID:	*"It is the desire of his heart to be an author."*

*R*obert Louis Stevenson, born in 1850 in Edinburgh, Scotland, spent his early years in a cold, damp, north-facing apartment, alternately suffering with and recovering from colds and bronchitis. Little Robert Louis was cherished and idolized at home but spent difficult years in school, where he was described by a young friend as a "pathetic little mite standing by the door, solitary and appealing."

It was in November of 1856, at the age of six, that he

became an author, according to biographer, Rosaline Masson, when his uncle, David Stevenson, had offered his own children and his nephews a prize for the best history of Moses. Robert competed by dictating his story to his mother, to whom he dedicated his efforts, and won the family prize.

After this early success, young Robert Louis Stevenson's efforts were described in his mother's journal: "It is the desire of his heart to be an author." Her faith in his literary genius never wavered, according to Masson. As an adult, widely known for his literary genius by a much larger following, Robert Louis Stevenson recalls those weary nights of his sickly childhood and his mother's share in them in a poem "The Sick Child."

> O Mother, lay your hand upon my brow!
> Out in the city, sounds begin,
> Thank the kind God, the carts come in.

SOURCE:
Rosaline Masson, *Life of Robert Louis Stevenson* (New York: Frederick A. Stokes Co., 1923).

FAMOUS CHILD:	Marian Anderson
MOTHER'S NAME:	Anna D. Anderson
MAMA . . .	*realized that she was left alone to raise three girls, and knew that she had to have a support beyond herself.*

arian Anderson, born in 1902, spent her early childhood with a devoted mother and father in a neighborhood of extended family in South Philadelphia. Described as a life of "great joy," Marian remembered yearly trolley rides to the Barnum and Bailey circus with her two sisters, all sporting new clothes, on a day equal only to Easter Sunday in importance. Every Sunday the family went to church and it was there that Marian first began to sing publicly, performing in her first concert outside of church as an eight year old.

At ten, Marian's world was shattered when her father died, leaving his young family behind. Anna Anderson and her daughters moved into her mother and father's house, a large three-story home with two cousins and an aunt. Anna, a tiny and energetic woman who had enjoyed being home for her children, now went to work to support the household. Marian related that "Mother's religion makes her believe that she will receive what it is right for her to have if she is good and conscientious in her faith. If it does not come, it is because He has not considered it right for her. She does not question."

As years went by, Marian took singing lessons and received increasing fame as well as money for her singing performances. The faith that she witnessed in her home did much to sustain her during difficult times as an adult obtaining the training necessary for a career. In 1939, when the Daughters of the American Revolution denied her, a black woman, access to Washington's Constitution Hall for a concert, Eleanor Roosevelt arranged a concert for her on the steps of the Lincoln Memorial before an audience of seventy-five thousand.

She was the first black singer to perform at the Metropolitan Opera House in New York City, and in 1935, sang for Arturo Toscanini, who said that she had "a voice that comes once in a hundred years."

In the words of Marian Anderson, who dedicated her autobiography to her mother, "A great deal of what I am and what I have achieved I owe to her."

SOURCE:
Marian Anderson, *My Lord, What a Morning: An Autobiography* (New York: Viking Press, 1956).

FAMOUS CHILD:	Naomi Judd (Diana Ellen Judd)
MOTHER'S NAME:	Polly Judd
MAMA SAID:	*"Let the men run around trying to change the world. I just want to improve my family."*

*D*iana Ellen Judd, now known as Naomi Judd, grew up in Ashland, Kentucky, along the Ohio River, the first child of a gas-station owner and a housewife. Naomi's mother, Polly, was "always in the kitchen," according to Naomi; "her days were filled to the brim with domesticity." Quick to help or house relatives, she had few luxuries but never complained or stopped laughing. The Judd house was the "center of the neighborhood" with kids everywhere. Polly, having come from a "fractured background," survived and brought much comfort to her family with the help of the deepest source of her identity—her God, according to Naomi.

Many years later, in 1983, Naomi and her daughter, Polly's granddaughter, Wynonna, performed for RCA and became country music's Duet of the Year for the next eight years. They won six Grammys and sold over fifteen million albums in 1991, when suddenly Naomi, threatened with life-threatening liver disease, was forced to retire from show business, leaving her daughter to carry on her career alone. The faith demonstrated by Polly many years before sustained the family as Naomi, supported by both her mother and daughter, spent two quiet years recovering from her disease before it went into remission. In Naomi's song, "Love Can Build a Bridge," the last line summarizes this faith by suggesting that people can do anything if they believe in the power of God. In the words of Naomi, "I believe that music is the breath of God; I think it's a healer."

Polly Judd continues to live in the same house in Ashland, Kentucky, along the Ohio River that Naomi and Wynonna remember as children, holding her large, extended

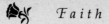

family together "like psychological glue." Polly was honored by her daughter and granddaughter as they sang and dedicated the first song they had ever learned to her, "The Sweetest Gift, a Mother's Smile."

SOURCE:
Naomi Judd and Bud Schaetzle, *Naomi Judd: Love Can Build a Bridge* (New York: Villard Books, 1993).

FAMOUS CHILD:	Kathie Lee Gifford (Kathryn Lee Epstein)
MOTHER'S NAME:	Joan Nancy Cuttell
MAMA SAID:	*"Nothing satisfied my heart like the Gospel of Jesus Christ."*

athie Lee's mother, Joan, a beautiful strawberry blond with blue eyes, grew up in a family that emigrated to Toronto from England in the mid-1800s. Losing her own mother at the age of two, she spent a lonely childhood and never experienced the home life she was later determined to give to her own children. "But I was fesity," Joan said. "I knew I was going to survive."

Kathie Lee grew up with her older brother and younger sister in an active, resourceful family that valued hard work and watched their pennies, and where "summers were idyllic." As a child, Kathie Lee remembers when her mother found her deep and abiding faith. She was watching a Billy Graham crusade alone when she "spontaneously knelt down in front of the TV set, asking Jesus to be the Lord and Savior of her life." Although Joan had found comfort in prayer throughout a troubled childhood, her faith had now became a more formal one.

Kathie Lee, with a faith learned from her mother, participated in her Campus Crusade for Christ at Oral Roberts University, performed gospel music in the seventies, and now co-hosts the daily television show, *Regis and Kathie Lee*, where her spontaneous chatter with Regis Philbin and guests delights a large audience. Before she goes on the air each day she prays, " 'Lord, please help me today. Don't let me hurt anyone with my mouth.' Why do I pray? Because I never know what's going to pop out of my mouth."

SOURCE:
Kathie Lee Gifford with Jim Jerome, *I Can't Believe I Said That: An Autobiography* (New York: Pocket Books, 1991).

FAMOUS CHILD:	**Danny Thomas (Muzyad Yakhoob, then Amos Jacobs)**
MOTHER'S NAME:	**Margaret Jacobs**
MAMA SAID:	*"Please, God, spare him and I will vow to you. I vow that I will beg pennies from door to door for a whole year to give to the poor."*

anny Thomas was the fifth son of ten children born to poor immigrants from Becheri, in the mountains of Lebanon. Becheri, part of the Ottoman Empire, was ruled by the Turks and its residents spoke Aramaic, the language of Christ. Margaret Jacobs emigrated to Toledo, Ohio, at the age of ten, and later gave birth to Danny on the family farm in Deerfield, Michigan, in 1914. A kind, honest, and loving mother who cooked, tended the garden, and mothered ten children, she couldn't read or write in any language. She went to church daily and, according to her son, "had a faith in God I've never seen matched anywhere."

Margaret spoke these words during the illness of Danny's six-month-old baby brother who was bitten by a rat as he lay in his crib. The doctors did their best but the youngster was close to death. Upon his subsequent recovery, Margaret Jacobs, true to her word, walked the streets of Toledo daily for one year, begging pennies from door to door. Many years later, Danny Thomas, by then the famous entertainer, said, "I'm sure that that memory of her was the chief reason why I later kept my own vow to St. Jude when I made it."

Danny made his own vow in Detroit shortly after the birth of daughter, Marlo. Times were tough, he had a family to support, he was known around the city as "a pretty fair fifty-dollar-a-week M.C.," but now he was nearing forty. Clearly he needed more money. Remembering a drunk years ago who had told him that his wife was cured of cancer by his own prayer to St. Jude, Danny made his vow. If his prayers were answered and he was shown a way to support his young family, he would build a shrine to St.

Jude. Years later, after a move to Chicago that led to his increasingly successful career as a performer, Danny Thomas remembered the vow made years before. In a meeting with Samuel Cardinal Stritch of Chicago, Danny conceived his shrine—a research hospital for catastrophic children's diseases. It was "more than ten years before I would see St. Jude's materialize in stone and mortar," Danny added in his biography.

Danny began his career as a character actor in commercials and radio drama in Chicago, before his starring role in *Make Room for Daddy*, which ran on television prime time for eleven years. Launching his own personal crusade, he founded the world-famous St. Jude Children's Research Hospital in Memphis, Tennessee, dedicated in 1962. At the end of a long and successful career and in the fifty-fourth year of his marriage to Rose Marie, Danny shared, "Accidental success? It happens to me all the time. My faith has a lot to do with it, too."

SOURCE:
Danny Thomas with Bill Davidson, *Make Room for Danny* (New York: G. P. Putnam's Sons, 1991).

FAMOUS CHILD:	Diana Ross
MOTHER'S NAME:	Ernestine Moten Ross
MAMA SANG:	*"I sing because I'm happy,* *I sing because I'm free.* *His eye is on the sparrow* *And I know He watches me."*

*E*rnestine Ross, born the youngest of twelve children, was a devoted, kind, loving mother who had an "incredible dignity about her. Times were tough," according to her daughter, Diana Ross. "We were a handful. We knew that she loved us completely." Diana shares that her mother always sang the old gospel hymn, "His Eye Is on the Sparrow." "It was my mother's prayer or her protection for us. Mama gave this song to me."

Ernestine kept their Detroit apartment immaculately

clean to protect her family from the bugs and rats that frequented other apartments in the building. The apartment, filled with music from the radio, phonograph, or spirituals sung by Ernestine, was a happy and secure place for her children. The bright yellow kitchen was the family gathering place with Ernestine, her devoted sister, and the family's "second mom," Bea, holding court.

Ernestine's husband worked two or three jobs and she did odd jobs to help support the family. One was a job at the movie theater which Diana describes as "the most magical place in the world," and which exposed her to some of the entertainers she would get to know as an adult.

Diana Ross signed with Motown records in 1961, sang with the Supremes, and has been at the top of her profession for three decades. Her portrayal of Billie Holiday in *Lady Sings the Blues* won her an Oscar nomination. Before her performances, she quietly prays:

> Thank you, God, for this wonderful life.
> Thank you for your grace and your blessings,
> Please keep your eye on this sparrow.

SOURCE:
Diana Ross, *Secrets of a Sparrow: Memoirs* (New York: Villard Books, 1993).

FAMOUS CHILD:	**Johnny Cash**
MOTHER'S NAME:	**Reba Cash**
MAMA SAID:	*"I don't know exactly what He has in mind, but God has His hand on you."*

*J*ohnny Cash, born on a Kingsland, Arkansas, farm in 1932, worked hard as a child to help his family make ends meet. His father, "dedicated to providing for his family," never had to receive government money or accept handouts even during the Depression, while the family struggled to raise enough vegetables, chickens, and cotton to pay the bills. When the family wasn't farming, their time was spent in song—both at the Church of God where there were many musical instruments to accompany the singing, and at home where a battery-operated Sears Roebuck radio continued the musical inspiration. "Those songs carried me away," said Johnny, "and they gave me a taste of heavenly things."

Reba Rivers Cash, whose father had "led the singing" at a Methodist Church for over forty years, thought that her young son, Johnny, resembled him in many ways, but remained perplexed that Johnny's high tenor voice was not the low, booming voice of her dad's. One day, at sixteen, Johnny returned home after a day of chopping wood, and as he walked into the kitchen, he sang softly to himself. His mother, eyes full of tears, said, "You sound exactly like my daddy." At sixteen, Johnny Cash's voice had changed to a rich, low, booming sound, prompting his mother's proud comment and declaration of faith.

Johnny Cash and his family experienced their share of heartbreak. Jack Cash, Johnny's adored older brother, died suddenly when Johnny was twelve. As an adult, Johnny Cash struggled with drug addiction for seven long years, spending periods of time in prison, prompting his brother Roy to comfort his mother by saying, "He's been through the fire for a special reason." Reba Rivers Cash responded,

"I've always said that God had His hand on John, and He still does." This "special reason" is apparent to Johnny Cash's many fans who have witnessed the country singer and guitar player sing his first hit in 1956, "I Walk the Line," and receive three Grammy Awards for his efforts. With the same strong faith exhibited by his mother, Johnny Cash explains, "my story has a lot to do with God. An awful lot."

SOURCE:
Johnny Cash, *Johnny Cash: Man in Black* (Zondervan Publishing Corp., 1975).

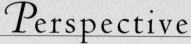

Perspective

Rachel Carson

John Cleese

Eric Sevareid

David Brenner

W. C. Fields

Ronald Reagan

Bob Hope

Will Rogers

Doris Day

Jack Lemmon

Harry S. Truman

Meryl Streep

Babe Didrikson Zaharias

Shirley Temple Black

Laura Ingalls Wilder

Norman Rockwell

Perspective

🎗 A sense of perspective gives us a clear and focused view of events, people, and choices and helps us lead a life of purpose and direction. In any number of ways, by methods subtle and overt, mothers play a central role in their children's ability to have a broader view of life. In the following stories, a well-developed motherly perspective ultimately translated into her child's future fame and fortune.

One type of perspective is the ability to see value and beauty in the little things in life, to appreciate life's hidden mysteries. As early as the age of two, Maria McLean Carson took her daughter Rachel for long walks along the Allegheny River, sharing her knowledge and appreciation of its beauty. Guided by her childhood perspective, Rachel Carson perceived and communicated threats to the environ-

ment to an unknowing public, leading to a lifetime of con-
servation advocacy with the birth of her book *Silent Spring*.

Humor is another aspect of perspective. In a world where
a multitude of sobering events assail us on a minute-by-
minute basis, humor permits us to maintain equilibrium and
keep a distance that makes it easier to deal with life. David
Brenner received this gift from his mother. Soft-spoken and
accepting, David's "best sweetheart" Stelle Brenner was central to her family of everyday comedians while they kept
trying through humor to keep the sun shining in a poor,
tough neighborhood in Philadelphia. And earlier in Philadelphia, Kate Dukinfield chatted with friends and observed
people pass by in her busy neighborhood. Later, inside, she
impersonated them to the delight of her young son, who
watched, learned, and used this style later in his own career
as comedian W. C. Fields.

Perspective has another dimension as well. Make the
best lemonade you can with the lemons life gives you, and
it will often lead to something better. The mothers of Ronald
Reagan and Doris Day saw past challenging life events.
Each mother possessed a positive perspective that became
a trademark of their child's future success.

Nelle Reagan's ambitious son Ronald came home with a new college degree looking for the elusive good job during the Depression. He accepted a job as a sporting-goods department manager, vowing to be the best they had ever seen. Nelle Reagan later observed, "If you hadn't had that problem back then, then this better thing that did happen wouldn't have happened to you." Alma Kappelhoff was thrilled as her young, talented daughter danced her way toward a Hollywood career. Her daughter's serious car accident, however, at the age of twelve temporarily shattered this dream. During her daughter's long recuperation, Alma maintained a hopeful attitude and encouraged her to focus on singing instead. Her daughter, who we now know as Doris Day, eventually went on not only to sing, but also to dance her way to stardom.

Clara Sevareid, mother of Eric, had her own ideas about education. Concerned that her small farming community was giving Eric a narrow perspective on the world, Clara exposed her young son to classical music and the writings of Shakespeare. Eric Sevareid's informed perspective, revealed in his nightly television news commentary, served Eric and his nation well as he interpreted the dizzying events of the Vietnam era for a frequently perplexed public.

It is the fortunate child who receives motherly perspective early in life. Armed with this virtue, a child is free to develop a balanced and focused view of the world, as the following stories illustrate.

FAMOUS CHILD:	Rachel Carson
MOTHER'S NAME:	Maria McLean Carson
MAMA SAID:	*"Listen, Rachel. Do you hear that?"*

For Rachel Carson, born in 1907 in Springdale, Pennsylvania, along the Allegheny River, there was a childhood full of things to see and wildlife to observe. Rachel's lifelong knowledge and respect for nature began on long walks with her mother, Maria Carson, originally trained as a teacher and pianist, who would exclaim at each sound young Rachel heard and each new thing she saw. These frequent walks imparted a powerful message to her young, bright daughter. This story of sharing, according to biographer Philip Sterling, "began with the song of a meadowlark."

During the Depression, Rachel pursued her master's degree in marine zoology at Pittsburgh's Pennsylvania College for Women, then wrote a nature column for the *Baltimore Sun* before she published her first book, *Under the Sea Wind*, in 1941, which her mother helped her type. Rachel Carson was best known, however, for her literary masterpiece *Silent Spring*, in which she described in detail a world of nature which she strongly believed to be threatened by the results of man's intervention. The sights, sounds, knowledge, and perspective derived from these childhood observations with her mother, Maria McLean Carson, led to the revelations in *Silent Spring*, which haunted a nation and gave birth to a generation's renewed concern with environmental issues.

SOURCE:
Philip Sterling, *Sea and Earth: The Life of Rachel Carson* (Thomas Y. Crowell Co., 1970).

FAMOUS CHILD:	John Cleese
MOTHER'S NAME:	Muriel Cross Cleese
MAMA SAID:	*"Well, two of his cousins were furriers."*

The Monty Python troupe, with their weekly humor program on BBC in the 1970s, gave the world a dose of humorous perspective on government, politics, religion, family life, and a lot more. Pythoner John Cleese found his sense of humor and perspective at home with his mother. He recalled the above quote as an early example of his mother's brand of wit, given in response to his frequent question about whether he had any Jewish blood in him, so large was his father's nose.

She demonstrated her wit to us all in radio ads for his film *Life of Brian*, which featured Mrs. Cleese pleading with people to see the film so she "won't have to go into an old people's home." Further evidence of the perspective imparted to Cleese by his mom comes in his observation that, in tribute to her, upon her death she will be "stuffed and put in a glass case in our front hall."

In his biography of the British comedian, Jonathan Margolies postulated that most humorists have dominant mothers. Cleese himelf noted that all of the Monty Python team came from mother-centered families.

SOURCE:
Jonathan Margolies, *Cleese Encounters* (New York: St. Martin's Press, 1992).

FAMOUS CHILD:	**Eric Sevareid**
MOTHER'S NAME:	**Clara Hougen Sevareid**
MAMA DID:	*Rather than introduce her children to reading and music through nursery rhymes, Clara started them out on Shakespeare and classical music.*

*G*rowing up in tiny Velva, North Dakota, Sevareid benefited from a mother who espoused high aspirations for her children. Sevareid's biographer, Raymond Schroth, noted that Mrs. Sevareid once said she "feared and hated the fact that wheat so absolutely controlled our lives as our solace and our challenge." As a cultivated woman from an intellectual family, she saw it as her personal responsibility to overcome the limited view of life in the small farming town and to give her young son a broader perspective of the world.

The thoughtful and well-spoken television news commentator was hired for CBS in 1939 by Edward R. Murrow. Like his mentor, Sevareid became a champion of the value of broadcast journalism. Each day during the troubled decades of the 60s and 70s, Walter Cronkite turned to Sevareid for a sense of perspective in the day's issues. Sevareid credited his mother for his love of books and scholarly thinking that gave him the required foundation for his focused analysis.

SOURCE:
Raymond A. Schroth, *The American Journey of Eric Sevareid* (South Royalton, VT: Steerforth Press, 1995).

FAMOUS CHILD:	David Brenner
MOTHER'S NAME:	Stelle Brenner
MAMA SAID:	*"Every boy has some Peck's bad boy in him. David's problem is he had too much in him, but he really is an angel—when he sleeps."*

*I*n the foreword of David's book, he states that "Everyone has parents, but not everyone, if he or she were given a choice, would choose these same persons to be their family. As a child I was also surrounded by fantastic aunts and uncles. This is real luck!"

Surrounded by a father who was "always looking for a shortcut to fame and fortune," a sister who had an "uncanny ability that opened a lot of doors in life," an aunt who had a "twinkle in her eye and a combination of wisdom and perspective in her constant chatter," and a mother who was "my best sweetheart," David received the perspective necessary to become one of our leading humorists. Gentle, soft-spoken Stelle loved to read, do ceramics, and sew but hated to cook, according to her son. Much of the family humor centered around stories of Stelle's failures in the kitchen, giving rise to a perspective that made everyday life the foundation for his humor. Growing up in a "poor, tough, big-city neighborhood" in Philadelphia, David learned early from his family that there was true value in cultivating a sense of humor. "Sunshine," David explains, "rarely shines in such places. Amid all that was wrong in those dark streets and back alleys, there were stockpiles of laughter and many crucial benefits."

Thirteen-year-old David, buoyed by the legacy of his family's humorous perspective on everyday events, clearly had translated this into much larger goals when he wrote to his mother, "I'm shooting for the highest star up there, Mom, because, if I miss, the worst that will happen is I'll fall to the moon, but if I aim only for the moon and miss, I'm liable to land right back here in the neighborhood."

SOURCE:
David Brenner, *Soft Pretzels with Mustard* (New York: Arbor House, 1983).

Kate had a habit of chatting with passersby from her Philadelphia home's doorway, while impersonating them in asides to her family. Then, after they had moved along, she would further mimic them with great comic skill. Field's biographer, Robert Lewis Taylor, claims that W. C. learned his trademark muttered asides from his mother, who gave the above response after seeing him act out the motherly routine in a New York show years later.

Fields's son, Ronald, also noted her gifted sense of humor and observation, noting she regularly ridiculed her English-born husband's Cockney accent, which Fields probably both inherited and copied in his own extravagant nasal drawl.

Biographer Taylor credits Fields's ability to communicate perspective through the humor in ordinary life to W. C.'s early struggles with things like hunger, cold, bartenders, and police. This, along with his careful observance of his mother's wit, were major factors in shaping his art, which came to be displayed in movies with titles such as *Never Give a Sucker an Even Break, My Little Chickadee,* and *You Can't Cheat an Honest Man.*

SOURCES:

Robert Lewis Taylor, *W. C. Fields—His Follies and Fortunes* (New York: Doubleday and Co., 1949).

Ronald J. Fields, *W. C. Fields by Himself: His Intended Autobiography with Hitherto Unpublished Letters, Notes, Scripts and Articles and Commentary* (Prentice Hall, 1973).

FAMOUS CHILD:	Ronald Reagan
MOTHER'S NAME:	Nelle Wilson Reagan
MAMA SAID:	*"If you hadn't had that problem back then, then this better thing that did happen wouldn't have happened to you."*

$\mathcal{J}$n the midst of the Depression in 1932, the northwestern Illinois town of Dixon was suffering. Many families had "lost land to crushing debt, the cement plant had closed, and the downtown had boarded-up shops," former president Ronald Reagan related in his memoirs. Young Reagan had a new college diploma and a fervent desire to get a good job. However, soon after being rejected by a Chicago radio station for a job as an announcer, Reagan headed back to Dixon, totally discouraged.

Before long a job came up in the new Montgomery Ward store in town for someone with a sports background to head the sporting-goods department, a modest job for someone with a college degree and lots of ambition.

Reagan wrote that his mother "had a sense of optimism that ran as deep as the cosmos" and believed that "everything in life happens for a purpose." Nelle's positive attitude served her son Ronald Reagan well. He soon decided that he would be the best sporting-goods department manager they had ever seen. Armed with a healthy perspective and a good attitude, Ronald Reagan went on to succeed as a film actor and as president of the United States, inspiring others with the positive outlook his mother had demonstrated so many years before.

SOURCE:
Ronald Reagan, *An American Life* (New York: Simon & Schuster, 1990).

FAMOUS CHILD:	Leslie "Bob" Hope
MOTHER'S NAME:	Avis Townes Hope
MAMA SAID:	*"The poolroom is just part of growing up. Don't worry about Leslie. He'll turn out fine."*

*B*ob Hope, born Leslie Hope in a London suburb in 1903, immigrated to Cleveland through Ellis Island with his family four years later. As one of seven sons during the depression of 1907, Bob and his family scraped through by taking in boarders and accepting a series of odd jobs. Avis Hope, the petite, energetic daughter of a Welsh sea captain, was fiercely determined to guide her seven sons to success. She remained optimistic during difficult times, and according to Hope's biographers, "walked on the bright side of life."

At the age of twelve, Bob was a familiar figure around Cleveland pool halls as he struggled to win enough money from his equally poor friends, prompting Aunt Louise to comment that Bob would turn out to be a loafer. Avis "had great faith in the goodness of her sons," according to Bob's brother Jack, and her quick retort set Aunt Louise straight. Bob remembers: "The Hope family was a tightly knit group, ready to stand as a unit against any threat to its security, ready to fight individually for one another in any crisis whatsoever."

The ambitious young Bob Hope was never one to shirk making a dollar. He worked in a bakery, butcher shop, soda fountain, shoe store, golf course, and newspaper stand. With the proceeds he would scurry off to the cinema, where according to Bob, "I sat in the dark for hours."

Avis Hope, with her cheerful perspective and fierce loyalty to her sons, knew what Aunt Louise at the moment did not, that this stage would pass and he would "turn out fine." From an early start in vaudeville at age twenty, Hope moved on to become a legend in theater, movies, and television for seven more decades.

SOURCES:

Charles Thompson, *Bob Hope: Portrait of a Superstar* (New York: St. Martin's Press, 1981).

Joe Morella, Edward Z. Epstein, and Eleanor Clark, *The Amazing Careers of Bob Hope* (New Rochelle, NY: Arlington House, 1973).

FAMOUS CHILD:	**Will Rogers**
MOTHER'S NAME:	**Mary America Schrimsher**
MAMA SAID:	*"Willie has a good idea. That'll make it sweeter. It'll be the best bread we ever had."*

One day young Will Rogers got the bright idea to place his bare foot into a pan of yeast that was sitting unattended on the floor of the family's kitchen. His mother, who had a natural kindness and a talent for putting life's little disasters into proper perspective, found a way to turn her son's messy misstep into an occasion for tongue-in-cheek praise.

Born to Clem and Mary Rogers when they were both forty, Will was the youngest of four and the only boy. Part

Cherokee Indian, he grew up on a ranch in Indian territory, later to become Oklahoma, and spent much of his childhood on horseback while learning to rope. His three older sisters and both parents, according to biographer Ben Yagoda, "were prepared to give him anything he wanted—and forgive him any mischief."

Referring to his mother years after her death, Will stated that "My own folks have told me what little humor I have comes from her." His wife Betty said that Will "cried when he told me about her death many years later. It left him a lonely, lost feeling that persisted long after he was successful and famous."

From the early 1920s until his premature death in a plane crash at the age of fifty-six, Will Rogers, the popular lecturer, storyteller, humorist, and satirist, was known to millions through his newspaper column, radio and film performances, and his top billing in the Ziegfeld Follies.

SOURCE:
Ben Yagoda, *Will Rogers: A Biography* (New York: Alfred A. Knopf, 1993).

FAMOUS CHILD:	Doris Day (Doris Kappelhoff)
MOTHER'S NAME:	Alma Sophia Kappelhoff
MAMA SAID:	*"What do the doctors say?" young Doris asked. Alma quickly responded, "You're going to be all right."*

*I*n her memoirs, Doris Day summarized her view of life with the words of the song "Que Sera Sera": "Whatever will be, will be, and I have made the best of it." Doris's philosophy complements her mother's advice—"You're going to be all right"—reflecting a sincere faith in her daughter's ability to overcome a childhood car accident that could easily have kept Doris Day out of the annals of entertainment history.

As a kindergartner living in a German community in

Evanston, Ohio, young Doris Kappelhoff took up dancing, which quickly became a dominant force in her life. In 1936, at the age of twelve, Doris and a boy from dancing school put together an act that was beginning to win contests and attract attention, so much so that Doris and her mother were going to move to Hollywood. It was then that disaster struck. While at a goodbye party, Doris and four friends decided to go out for hamburgers and shakes. On the way the car was hit by a train, shattering Doris's right leg and threatening to stop short the dancing career for which she had been studying and working. Once Doris regained consciousness, her first words were, "What about my dancing? What do the doctors say?" Alma knew that this was no time to tell Doris that her right leg was shattered and that the doctors were concerned that she might never dance again. She said, "You're going to be all right."

Alma's positive attitude made a profound impact during Doris's long convalescence. Instead of focusing on what Doris could not do, Alma guided her daughter toward an area in which she could succeed, singing. By the time Doris was able to abandon her crutches many months later, she had mastered the fundamentals of singing and went on not only to sing, but to walk, dance, and perform with the likes of Les Brown and Jimmy Dorsey. Later she traveled with Bob Hope and starred in a number of movies as Doris Day.

SOURCE:
A. E. Hotchner, *Doris Day: Her Own Story* (New York: William Morrow and Co., 1976).

FAMOUS CHILD:	Jack Lemmon
MOTHER'S NAME:	Mildred "Millie" Lemmon
MAMA SAID:	*"Are you kidding? Never again. I'm damned glad you came out all right." (when asked by young Jack if she planned to give him a brother or sister)*

*T*he Oscar-winning actor was raised in Boston by a prosperous mother gifted with a refined sense of humor and a perspective on life. Pretty, bright, and extroverted, Millie was the kind of woman who, in the words of Lemmon biographer Don Widener, "straight-armed reality with one-liners and perfectly mixed martinis." One night at a bridge party, when she was pregnant with Jack, she laughed off the clear physical signs of his impending birth only to have to make an emergency rush to the hospital in time to have Jack delivered in an elevator. A nurse, seeing the slightly jaundiced look of the premature infant, told the mother, "My, look at the little Lemmon."

Millie was very close to her only child, especially after difficulties in her marriage. When Jack portrayed a woman in the movie *Some Like It Hot*, another actor observed that Jack looked like his mother. Lemmon explained that he felt it was "sense memory," oberving, "Sometimes when you are faced with a scene in which you must evoke a particular emotion, you can draw from a parallel situation, something you've witnessed or experienced."

Lemmon's career has been marked by his ability to apply his own perspective to a variety of roles, ranging from the fastidious Felix in *The Odd Couple* comedy to serious dramatic roles, such as the alcoholic in *The Days of Wine and Roses*. Widener observes Jack's perspective by commenting, "Lemmon's scenes are alternatively funny, sad, wild, tender, adding up to the rollicking story of the boy with the face that any mother could love who became the man who had the grace to make a fool of himself and the talent to pull it off."

SOURCE:
Don Widener, *Lemmon* (New York: Macmillan Publishing Co., 1975).

MOTHER'S NAME: Martha E. Truman

MAMA SAID: *"One must always be cheerful.*
If asked how you were, you
were always to respond 'I'm
fine. And you?' . . . Keep troubles
to yourself."

H arry Truman's cousin, Ethel Noland, recalled that despite a difficult Missouri farm life and serious financial losses incurred by Harry's father in wheat futures, the Trumans didn't ask for handouts from anybody. After his father's death, when his mother nearly lost the family farm, her resourceful, positive, and independent son worked on his own to try to save it instead of spending time bemoaning the family fate.

Martha Truman studied art and music at the Baptist

Female College in Lexington, Missouri, at a time when many women were not formally educated. Throughout her life she valued art and books and passed these values to her son, who had read close to three thousand books by the time he was fourteen and who also played the piano. Described as "never deviating from her idea of what was right" and having "the finest set of values I have ever known" by Harry Truman's first cousin Ethel Noland, Martha Truman influenced her son with her perspective on many events throughout her son's life. At the age of eighty-eight, she was still sharing her perspective on the people around Truman. She was a "very good judge of people, her eyes were just as sharp as ever, and she never had any trouble sizing up who was going the right way and who was going the wrong way as far as I was concerned." This information often helped Truman decide who was truly trustworthy and who wasn't, a valuable source of information for a president of the United States.

Always one to tackle a difficult job, Truman described himself as "not worried about the job in the White House. Worrying never does you any good." Truman's solid values and propensity for hard work, coupled with his mother's cheerful, positive approach to life and foundation of sound principles, were a significant base upon which to build a career of leadership. His strong sense of independence, pragmatism, and responsibility were embodied in his famous slogan, printed on a sign on his desk, THE BUCK STOPS HERE.

SOURCES:

David McCullough, *Truman* (New York: Simon & Schuster, 1992).

Merle Miller, *Plain Speaking: An Oral Biography of Harry S. Truman* (New York: G. P. Putnam's Sons, 1973).

FAMOUS CHILD:	Meryl Streep (Mary Louise Streep)
MOTHER'S NAME:	Mary Louise Streep
MAMA SAID:	*"All my friends at one point or another wanted to throw up their hands and leave and see if there was another way of doing their lives."*

eryl Streep, born in 1949, grew up in Summit, New Jersey, the oldest of three children and the daughter of an advertising-executive father and a mother who freelanced as an illustrator. Tall, awkward, and mature as a child, Meryl loved to show off in home movies, and at twelve, sang a solo "O Holy Night" in a Christmas concert at school, revealing a lovely coloratura soprano voice. The family invested in four years of voice lessons in Manhattan, only to have Meryl return happily to cheerleading, which she preferred. Later in high school, Meryl went to see Barbara Cook in *The Music Man*. "If I could locate the moment I was first bitten, that was it," said Meryl. After four years at Vassar, during which Meryl lived and performed, according to biographer Diana Maychick, within "a community of active, supportive women," Meryl went on to follow her acting career.

Soon Meryl Streep was offered a part in *Kramer vs. Kramer* as Dustin Hoffman's wife, Joanna, a woman who leaves her husband and son when the pressures of home and career prove too difficult. Meryl thought the part of Joanna as written was "too narrowly described" and "too evil." "We never understand why she walked out," Meryl told the moviemakers.

At this point, in trying to understand her movie role as Joanna, and the dilemma of this wife and mother, Meryl turned to her mother for insight. Could her own mother and her friends relate to such a character? Meryl was shocked by her mother's response but certain that if her own mother and her friends had occasionally entertained the same thought, that other woman might have as well. According to biographer Maychick, Meryl "saw Joanna Kramer as a muddled, unhappy woman on the brink of a nervous breakdown she knew would never come." The insight, from her mother, guided Meryl in portraying Joanna in a much more sympathetic way, prompting writer-director Robert Benton to say at the end of the filming, "You can literally do anything." Meryl won an Academy Award as supporting actress in 1979 for her efforts.

SOURCE:
Diana Maychick, *Meryl Streep: The Reluctant Superstar* (New York: St. Martin's Press, 1984).

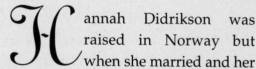

annah Didrikson was raised in Norway but when she married and her husband moved to Beaumont, Texas, for an oil-field job, it meant many changes and surprises. Many of the surprises came from her daughter Mildred. While Hannah was a skier and skater, she was not prepared for Mildred's athletic interest and prowess. The street was her playground, and playing one-on-one sports competitively with boys was the love of her life. Her neighborhood pranks, such as waxing the streetcar rails, were a problem for everyone on Doucette Street.

One time, Baby, as she was called, ripped a new dress and her angry mother started to chase her. Seeing her mother limping from a leg injury, she slowed down to be caught. The frustrated but fundamentally easy-going Hannah could not whip her but could only say of Babe, "I don't know where I got that 'ting." After several such incidents, according to biographer Susan Cayleff, the daughter began to value her "sweetly strict" mother's "gentle blend of discipline and amusement that greeted her shenanigans." She eventually recognized that her mother's temper was "slow to boil and quick to cool." Empowered by Hannah's love and perspective, Babe (as the media later labeled her in comparing her to Babe Ruth) began to focus her efforts on positive accomplishments and by high school saw as her goal in life becoming the "greatest athlete."

In 1932 she won two gold medals in track and field at the Olympics. Known as the Texas Tomboy, she was active in many sports but was best known for her golfing skills. She won the Associated Press Female Athlete of the Year six times and was a cofounder and director of the Ladies

Professional Golf Association. In 1945, when she was in the finals of a major golf tournament, she learned that Hannah was dying from a heart attack. Upon hearing from her sister that "Your momma wants you to finish the tournament," Babe continued and won. She later recalled she was inspired by her mother who was her "best friend . . . admirer . . . and fan."

While her own grave marker in Beaumont, Texas, where she was buried in 1956, is inscribed with "It's not whether you won or lost, it's how you play the game," many who knew her best recall her earlier comment, "I don't see any point in playing the game if you don't win. Do you?"

SOURCE:
Susan Cayleff, *Babe: Life and Legend of Babe Didrikson Zaharias* (Champaigne: University of Illinois Press, 1995).

FAMOUS CHILD:	**Shirley Temple Black**
MOTHER'S NAME:	**Gertrude Krieger Temple**
MAMA SAID:	***"We intend to keep her natural and unspoiled, even if it costs us $10,000 per week."***

S hirley Temple, born in 1928, lived in a stucco bungalow in Santa Monica with her father, manager of a California Bank branch, and her mother, Gertrude. Gertrude, with jet black hair, fancied herself a ballerina during her youth, but instruction was much too expensive and dancing was considered frivolous by her self-disciplined and hard-working German-Irish parents. While at a ballroom-dancing studio taking lessons years later, Gertrude met her husband and Shirley's father, George, and both subsequently began a marriage that lasted sixty years.

Born with a dimple in her right cheek, Shirley at three days old produced one on the left, leaving her, in her own words, "balanced and ready." It wasn't long after starting dancing lessons at the age of three that she was "balanced and ready" for a major screen career, after being discovered by a director looking for two girls and ten boys for a series of movies for Universal. Soon came not only a two-year contract for twenty-six movies, but also offers of commercials, appearances, and the media attention which prompted Gertrude Temple's remark.

Shirley describes this early training as "no namby-pamby; our job was to master a craft. Lesson after lesson, the dance routines were drilled and repeated. There were no shortcuts. Despite my initial resistance, Mother's knack for making a joy of obligatory behavior was a blessing."

During the Depression, Shirley Temple's movies fascinated America. She retired from films in 1949, and as an adult became politically active on behalf of the Republican party. Now Shirley Temple Black, she was appointed delegate to the United Nations General Assembly in 1969, U.S.

ambassador to Ghana in 1974, U.S. chief of protocol in 1976, and ambassador to Czechoslovakia in 1989.

Shirley's successful transition to adulthood was built upon the perspective and self-discipline learned from her mother. Unlike Shirley Temple, most child stars are unable to attain this kind of success as adults. In 1988, Shirley Temple "lovingly" dedicated her autobiography to her mother.

SOURCE:
Shirley Temple Black, *Child Star* (New York: McGraw-Hill, 1988).

Laura Ingalls Wilder was born in 1867 in the Big Woods of Wisconsin as America was just recovering from the Civil War. At the age of eighteen months, Laura and her family, looking for opportunity, moved west by covered wagon to the prairie—Indian Territory—now known as Kansas. They experienced threats from Indians, malaria, whooping cough, and scarlet fever, prompting their return to the Big Woods and later to the flat fertile prairie town of Plum Creek, Minnesota, in 1874, the year the town was founded. There the family was among the early settlers who started the first church and first school. Throughout her childhood, Laura enjoyed making maple-leaf hats for her dolls, hearing her father play the fiddle, sewing samplers, giving her dolls tea parties, and reading the Bible while experiencing a happy childhood. Her memories included the smells of the bonfires and spring flowers on the prairie; the sounds of her dad's fiddle and the covered-wagon wheels hitting the dirt road; the sight of a hayfield and the angle of the sun. She remembered clearly her life as a pioneer girl.

Mother, Caroline Quiner, took her teacher's exam three months past her sixteenth birthday, taught on the prairie before marriage, and knew that to succeed, her young daughters needed the perspective and knowledge derived from an education. Devoted to her husband and children, Caroline made a pleasant, loving, and solid home in the midst of change, and steadfastly pursued education for her children.

Laura Ingalls went on to marry Almanzo Wilder, and to live on a farm in the Missouri Ozarks, raise a daughter Rose, and write for the local paper. After the deaths of her father, mother, and siblings, Laura, melancholic and lost in her memories of the past, was determined that her family and their memories must not be lost. At her daughter Rose's urging, Laura sat down at the age of sixty-three with pencil and paper in a corner of her study and put on paper the happy memories and stories of her childhood.

Laura saw a "madness in the cities, a frenzy in the struggling crowds" and felt strongly that "at long last I am beginning to learn that it is the sweet, simple things of life that are the real ones after all." With this perspective, one initiated much earlier by her mother, Laura Ingalls Wilder, at sixty-three, wrote the first of these stories, *Little House in the Big Woods,* published in 1931. The re-creation of these stories, in the television series *Little House on the Prairie* continues to delight people everywhere.

SOURCE:
Donald Zochert, *Laura: The Life of Laura Ingalls Wilder* (Chicago: Henry Regnery Co., 1976).

orman Rockwell, the renowned American illustrator whose realistic work was on the cover of over three hundred editions of the *Saturday Evening Post* magazine, was born in New York City in 1894. Norman's mother, Nancy Rockwell, was the daughter of a talented, although less-than-successful artist, a father who often had to paint houses to support his family of twelve children. Nancy, disillusioned by her father's failure to provide for the family with the fruits of his artistic efforts, implored her son to be proud not only of her mother's English heritage but also of the art profession in general. It was her hope that Norman would be proud of his talent, and unlike her father, would do well enough to support himself, and accept nothing less.

In support of her English heritage, she named her son Norman Percevel after a distant ancestor who reportedly kicked Guy Fawkes down the stairs of the Tower of London after he allegedly tried to blow up the House of Lords. She made Norman wear a black armband for six weeks after the death of Queen Victoria.

While Nancy suffered from a long series of illnesses, she continued to encourage her son's early art. Rockwell recalled that his father would often read Charles Dickens to the family while young Norman would illustrate the images of Dickens' fully described characters. Rockwell states in his autobiography, "I think I always wanted to be an artist."

Despite a childhood image of himself as "a long skinny beanpole without the beans," he had the perspective from Nancy to be proud of his profession and to realize that his talent could give meaning and subsequent success to his life. He left high school at age sixteen to go to art school full-time and took a job as a magazine illustrator. He noted that illustration was "a profession with a great tradition, a profession I could be proud of. I guess my temperament and abilities were the other part."

Eventually, Norman Rockwell, illustrator of American family life over several generations, concluded, "Being somebody to my parents . . . meant a lot to me. I wasn't a rebel." With a pride in his profession learned from his mother and a disciplined approach to work, Norman Rockwell supported his family well.

SOURCE:
Norman Rockwell as told to Tom Rockwell, *Norman Rockwell: My Adventures as an Illustrator* (New York: Harry N. Abrams, 1994).

Responsibility

Henry Wadsworth Longfellow

John Fitzgerald Kennedy

Mark Twain

Dr. Benjamin Spock

David Letterman

Barbara Bush

Lauren Bacall

Warrick Dunn

Barbara Lavallee

Patsy Cline

Louisa May Alcott

Harry Houdini

Responsibility

Mothers who foster responsibility in their children guide them to take charge of their lives, to answer for their conduct, and to account for their actions. Responsible children make better decisions. Better decisions make successful people.

As the following anecdotes suggest, responsibility is best taught by example. Rose Kennedy knew the value of this method well. Her philosophy: "Bring up the oldest one the way you want them all to go." The result? Her first son, Joseph, Jr., served as an example for her other ultimately famous and successful children to follow. Dr. Benjamin Spock's mother regularly praised her oldest son for his care of his younger siblings. Dr. Spock learned responsibility from her, shared it with his siblings, and eventually based his entire career on it. His book *Baby and Child Care* taught millions of couples to be responsible parents and role models to their children. Louisa May Alcott wrote not only to help with family finances, but also to overcome her mother's discouragement about her own role as a woman and the lack of the existence of opportunities for women.

The mothers of David Letterman and Samuel Clemens turned their rebellious, energetic, and independent children into responsible and successful adults, while at the same time enabling their childhood spirit to infuse their adult sense of humor. Samuel Clemens's mother, Jane, expressed true frustration in watching her accident-prone young son trip and fall through an adventurous childhood, worried that he would not live to be an adult. Under her guidance, he not only grew up to be responsible but also the author of numerous childhood tales of adventure, such as *The Adventures of Tom Sawyer* and *Huckleberry Finn* under the name of Mark Twain. Dorothy Letterman had a problem. Her bright, energetic son David's antics conflicted with her midwestern conservative values. Once David found a speech class in high school in which he could excel and which led to a specific career, he finally had a goal. Dave's burning desire for a radio-television career, accompanied by a personal responsibility much like his mother's, led to his eventual success.

Honesty is another dimension of responsibility. Miguel de Cervantes, the sixteenth-century Spanish writer, said, "Honesty is the best policy"—to which the philosopher Immanuel Kant added two centuries later, "Honesty is better than policy." When a mother confronts a child with dishonest behavior, the lesson is rarely forgotten. Natalie Bacall caught her eleven-year-old daughter, Lauren, with a pencil box for which she had not paid. Natalie promptly marched her young daughter back to the five and dime to confess and to return the item, to her daughter's great humiliation. Lauren Bacall "never forgot this incident nor was it ever followed by another like it."

When a mother provides a climate of openness and acceptance, a child is more likely to be honest and thereby take responsibility for her actions. Pauline Pierce knew this well. When her daughters went out on dates, she stayed awake until they got home. Both daughters respected her and would tell her of their evening. Pauline also know that late at night, after an evening of fun, her daughters were more apt to "tell all." They often did. As First Lady, one of her daughters, Barbara Bush, modeled honesty and responsibility to an admiring public.

William Yeats said, in *The Coming of Wisdom with Time*, "In dreams begins responsibility." The mothers in this chapter, from Rose Kennedy to Dorothy Letterman, helped their children to become responsible adults and to achieve their dreams. The world is the richer for it.

FAMOUS CHILD:	Henry Wadsworth Longfellow
MOTHER'S NAME:	Hither Zilpah Wadsworth Longfellow
MAMA SAID:	*"I should really be pleased to have a letter from you once a term. The novelty would be quite delightful. Do you not love to write prose? Seriously, not a day passes that I do not think of my absent sons, nor do I ever forget them in my daily petitions to that Being who can alone protect us."*

*T*he mother of young Henry, who was a sophomore at Bowdoin College in 1824, expresses a typical mother's lament about college-age youth. Henry Wadsworth actually did write frequently to his mother, often to complain about the lack of heat and other living conditions in the room that he and his brother shared at the home of a local clergyman. His mother, while reminding her son of his responsibility to write, also expressed concern that this frosty atmosphere might prevent the proper expansion of his ideas and that "the muses will not visit you."

SOURCE:
Samuel Longfellow, ed., *Life of Henry Wadsworth Longfellow* (University Press, John Wilson & Son, 1886).

FAMOUS CHILD:	John F. Kennedy
MOTHER'S NAME:	Rose Kennedy
MAMA SAID:	*"Most important was to bring up the oldest one the way you want them all to go. If the oldest one comes in and says good night to his parents or says his prayers in the morning, the younger ones think that's the thing to do and they will do it."*

*R*ose Kennedy needed a lot of help to raise a family of six while maintaining an active social life. Her tip on child-rearing is one that many 1990s mothers might take to heart as they deal with the consequences of maintaining a professional career and raising a family.

Rose was a very proactive mother who fostered faith, responsibility, and organization in her children. These lessons apparently found willing ears. Each of her sons pursued political careers, perhaps spurred on by the interest shown by oldest son, Joseph. When Joe, Jr. died at an early age, Jack became the political role model for Robert and Teddy. Jack Kennedy once credited her with teaching him many lessons that prepared him for the presidency. He said, "There's no way you can prepare for the presidency. The only things I ever learned from anybody that might have helped were some of the early things I learned from my mother."

In her 1974 autobiography, *Times to Remember*, Rose wrote, "I would much rather be known as the mother of a great son or a great daughter than the author of a great book or the painter of a great masterpiece."

SOURCES:

Ralph G. Martin, *Hero for Our Time: An Intimate Story of the Kennedy Years* (New York: Macmillan Publishing Co., 1983).

Thomas Reeves, *A Question of Character: A Life of John Fitzgerald Kennedy* (New York: Free Press, 1991).

FAMOUS CHILD:	**Mark Twain (Samuel Clemens)**
MOTHER'S NAME:	**Jane Lampton Clemens**
MAMA SAID:	*"He drives me crazy with his didoes [antics] when he is in the house, and when he is out of it I am expecting every minute someone will bring him home dead."*

Clearly Jane Clemens faced an uphill battle teaching her rambunctious son the value of responsibility. Little Sam's escapades led all who loved him to worry, and according to biographer John Lauber, he "nearly drowned more than once, walked in his sleep, and would run away, usually toward the river." Summertime would find Sam at his Uncle John's farm, where one of the slaves, Old Uncle Dan'l, told ghost stories by firelight; homemade swings broke when a child was "forty feet in the air"; rattlers were killed, and harmless snakes collected in order to tease mothers and sisters. Twenty-five years later a Hannibal, Missouri, acquaintance inquired of Mark Twain "if you still climb out on the roof of the house and jump from the third-story windows."

Jane Clemens, remembered for her love of people and animals, gave birth to Samuel in Florida, Missouri, in 1835. She frequently brought home stray cats—"They were out of luck and that is enough; they had to stay." One day in St. Louis, Jane Clemens witnessed a cartman who was abusing his horse with a whip; she took the whip away from him and then, according to her son, "made such a persuasive appeal in behalf of the ignorantly offending horse that he was tripped into saying he was to blame and volunteered a promise that he wouldn't ever abuse a horse again." Spontaneous and outgoing Jane Clemens took responsibility for those unable to defend theirselves, and this lesson did not go unnoticed by her son.

Mark Twain, in spite of his mother's concern, survived his early adventures to become a responsible adult and world-renowned author of *The Adventures of Tom Sawyer* and *Huckleberry Finn.*

SOURCES:

John Lauber, *The Making of Mark Twain* (New York: American Heritage Press, 1985).

Charles Neider, *The Autobiography of Mark Twain* (New York: Harper & Row, 1966).

FAMOUS CHILD:	**Dr. Benjamin Spock, M.D.**
MOTHER'S NAME:	**Mildred Louise Stoughton**
MAMA SAID:	*"Benny, you are the oldest and you should know better."*

*T*he large Spock family of New Haven grew at regular two-year intervals for many years, making Benjamin the eldest of six children, responsible at an early age for his younger siblings. During their summer vacation at a cottage in Vinalhaven, Maine, nine-year-old Benjamin spent most of his time changing diapers and giving bottles, making him "more of a parent than a brother" to the newest infant. Ben identified with his mother in her love of babies and took to heart her comment pleading for him to be more responsible. That, added an adult Dr. Benjamin Spock, was the "main influence in my decision, a dozen years later, to go into pediatrics."

Dr. Benjamin Spock became the first medical-school graduate to major in both pediatrics and psychoanalysis. This gave him a sound basis upon which to build his career as a self-described "parent guide" with the publication of his book *Baby and Child Care*. That book has helped educate three generations of young parents with its philosophy that a child's health involves more than just physical symptoms.

SOURCE:
Benjamin Spock, M.D. and Mary Morgan, *Spock on Spock: A Memoir of Growing Up with the Century* (New York: Pantheon Books, 1989).

FAMOUS CHILD:	David Letterman
MOTHER'S NAME:	Dorothy Letterman
MAMA . . .:	*worried that the silly dream her son David had of becoming a broadcaster would stand in the way of a more sensible career, such as engineering or accounting.*

*Y*oung David Letterman was a constant source of disruption in his Indiana household. Dave admitted to *TV Guide*, "The house I grew up in was nuts because I was there." Dave recalled that his mother often had to reprimand him at dinnertime with the threat, "All right David, if you can't behave, take your plate and eat outside." He had early problems with school and was a regular prankster. At an after-school supermarket job, he once stacked cans of merchandise to the ceiling in such a way that when one can was removed the entire wall would tumble down.

From his earliest years in Broad Ripple, Indiana, David Letterman dreamed of becoming a broadcaster. In her book on his life, Rosemarie Lennon wrote that the first thing Dave built when given his first erector set as a child was a microphone. And, she reports, "he didn't sing into it, but instead gave speeches, told jokes, read commercials or introduced guests." To his reserved midwestern mother, this became problematical when he obsessed on watching television, perhaps because his parents limited it. Inspired by his mother's doubt, but inculcated with her sense of responsibility, when David went to Ball State University and became a communications major, he finally focused his pent-up energy and responsibly worked toward a real life goal.

David of course has come to be known as a king of late-night television. However, biographer Rosemarie Lennon concludes that he strives to say in many ways, "See Mom, I have made something of myself. What I do for a living is not a foolish waste of time." The world had a chance to see this relationship first hand when Dave employed his mother as a special correspondent to his nightly *Late Show* during the Lillehammer Olympics in 1994. While her gentle, endearing manner captivated Letterman's viewers, to biographer Lennon, her presence was really only one more way for Dave to impress the doubting mother who had refused to give her full approval to his career. To a conservative mother with a nontraditional son like Dave, it might have been the only way.

SOURCE:
Rosemarie Lennon, *David Letterman: On Stage and Off* (New York: Pinnacle Books, 1994).

FAMOUS CHILD:	Barbara Bush
MOTHER'S NAME:	Pauline Pierce
MAMA SAID:	*"Poppy is a wonderful boy who comes from a special family."*

*T*his was the initial reaction from Barbara's mom Pauline, after hearing her sixteen-year-old daughter say that she had just met the "nicest, cutest boy" at a vacation dance in their hometown of Greenwich, Connecticut. Pauline valued honesty and knew that teens frequently hid parts of their lives from their parents. She valued the closeness that she and her daughters had and maintained a tradition of visiting with her daughters as soon as they got home from their dates.

In her memoirs, Barbara wrote that her mother would always ask her daughters to come to her bedside to tell about their evening's activities. According to Barbara, Mrs. Pierce said she couldn't fall asleep until hearing from each of her children. However, the First Lady suspected the real reason for the ritual was that mother was "smart enough" to know that at night children are more willing to "tell it all." Pauline's insistence on maintaining honest communication with her teenage daughters kept them close to her throughout their lives and fostered a strong sense of responsibility in her children.

Poppy, son of Connecticut Senator Prescott Bush, was to be Barbara's future husband, George Herbert Walker Bush, and later, president of the United States.

SOURCE:
Barbara Bush, *Barbara Bush: A Memoir* (New York: Charles Scribner's Sons, 1994).

FAMOUS CHILD:	Betty "Lauren" Bacall
MOTHER'S NAME:	Natalie Bacall
MAMA SAID:	*"Let this be a lesson to you, taking what isn't yours is stealing. It's against the law."*

This episode occurred when eleven-year-old Lauren stole a pencil case from a five-and-dime store and was forced by her mother to return to the store and confess her theft. In her 1978 autobiography, *By Myself*, Bacall noted that "I never forgot this incident nor was it ever followed by another like it." She learned that "facing a situation head on, was the only way to deal with anything." She concluded that "my mother gave me a solid foundation."

The two remained close throughout the actress's career as Lauren starred in numerous movies and Broadway shows. Her 1945 storybook marriage to actor Humphrey Bogart and the tragedy of Bogart's early death, in 1957, from cancer is well known. Natalie Bacall helped her daughter through the difficulties of that tragedy. Lauren recalls another motherly message: "Your family never lets you down—remember that. When all else is lost, you can always depend on the family."

Bacall, in summarizing the highlights of her career, states, "To respect one's work and to do it well, to risk something in life was more important than being a star. To never sell your soul—to have self-esteem—to be true—was most important of all." In her second autobiography, entitled *Lauren Bacall Now*, she states that "My mother was the most important influence in my life."

SOURCES:

Lauren Bacall, *Lauren Bacall, By Myself* (New York: Ballantine Books, 1978).

Lauren Bacall, *Lauren Bacall Now* (New York: Alfred A. Knopf, 1994).

FAMOUS CHILD:	**Warrick Dunn**
MOTHER'S NAME:	**Betty Dunn Smothers**
MAMA SAID:	***"The first child sets the tone."***

When Baton Rouge police-woman and single mother Betty Dunn Smothers gave this message to the eldest of her six children, she was probably focusing on the need to have someone in charge when she was required to work sixteen-hour shifts. However, the message took on greater significance when she was killed during a police investigation of a robbery at an all-night convenience store. Her son, Warrick, a local high-school football star, vowed at that moment "to keep caring for his younger siblings who regarded him as a father figure." He feared he might not be able to go to college to play football but might have to stay in Baton Rouge to care for the family. He was reminded by a friend of his mother's message that she would want him to set the tone by making something of himself.

The family was supported by the Baton Rouge community, where Betty had always given much of herself. She once said to a fellow football parent when asked if she worried about getting killed, "It's just something that could happen, and if it happens, I know you'll all look after my kids." One other supporter noted that because Betty, as a single mother, "pushed her kids to do something with themselves, look how many dads they all have."

Warrick Dunn did get to go to college. He received an athletic scholarship to Florida State University, where he quickly became a national collegiate football star. When FSU returned to Louisiana to play in the 1995 Sugar Bowl in New Orleans, just eighty miles from his mother's grave, he was asked what it meant to play there. He explained that he had looked up to the sky before the kickoff and said, "This one's for you." On his football gloves he had printed the word MOM. The fleet halfback proceeded to lead his team to victory and receive the Sugar Bowl's Most Valuable Player award. He concluded, "My mother prepared me for this my whole life."

SOURCE:
Johnette Howard, "Playing in Pain," *Sports Illustrated*, 28 August 1995.

FAMOUS CHILD:	Barbara Lavallee
MOTHER'S NAME:	Dorothy Koehler
MAMA . . .	*taught her children that women are the glue of society.*

*a*rtist/illustrator Barbara Lavallee grew up surrounded by women who can take care of themselves. She noted, "They keep things together, make celebrations happen, care for the emotional and physical needs of the family." Her parents, Dorothy Koehler and her minister husband Clarence, were proud of their own education and wanted their four daughters to attend college and to succeed. When Clarence died suddenly in 1957,

Dorothy had to go back to work to support her young family. Her daughter Barbara, who had been the family artist, often drawing the character *Sheena of the Jungle* for her sisters, did attend college where her strongest subject was life drawing.

Barbara said, "Mostly because of Mother, I never questioned my own ability to make a life for me and my kids after my divorce. Often Mother was my sounding board, always encouraging and supporting. I know that she is proud of what I do, though once she confessed that she herself could not stand the uncertainty of the variable income that an artist's life entails."

Barbara moved to Alaska where her art career blossomed. She is now secure as an artist and book illustrator. Her captivating characters have enabled her to sell millions of her illustrated books, many illustrations depicting women and children. She stated, "I do some men and kids in my painting, but seldom do a painting of just men. Women are so much more colorful."

She illustrated the Barbara Joose book, *Mama Do You Love Me?* in 1991. She said of the book, which depicted many different scenes of Alaskan native women with their children, "This book was an illustrator's dream—a universal concept couched in the trappings of a culture and people that continue to fascinate me after over twenty years of living in Alaska. I was both the mother and the little girl."

SOURCE:
Barbara Lavallee & B. G. Olson, *Barbara Lavallee's Painted Ladies and Other Celebrations* (Seattle: Epicenter Press, 1995).

FAMOUS CHILD:	**Virginia Patterson "Patsy" Cline**
MOTHER'S NAME:	**Hilda Patterson Hensley**
MAMA SAID:	*"I was 16 years old when Patsy was born. All my life I'd had hand-me-downs, but when she was born, she was mine. We grew up together. We were hungry together."*

Six days after Hilda Patterson married Sam Hensley in 1932 in Winchester, Virginia, their daughter was born. They named her Virginia Patterson Hensley after both families. Times were tough during the Depression in the rural Blue Ridge mountain area. The marriage was a difficult one with the father often abusing both mother and daughter.

A close bond developed between Hilda and her daughter. Patsy, as she came to be known, noted later, "my mother's love was unconditional." Young Patsy showed early signs of her talent, winning a local dance contest at age four and singing in many local settings. Hilda took over responsibility for her daughter by taking in sewing to make ends meet and often drove her teenage daughter to singing engagements, not getting home until after 3 A.M., only hours before she had to be at work herself.

Even after Patsy married Gerald Cline in 1953, Hilda and Patsy remained close, becoming almost like sisters. Patsy got her big break when she was invited to appear on the national *Arthur Godfrey Talent Scouts* show on CBS Radio in 1957. Accompanied by her mother to New York under the guise of being her sister, Patsy won the contest singing her later to-be-famous song, "Walking After Midnight." She received a record contract for the song, and became a regular on the Godfrey show before joining the Grand Ole Opry in 1960.

After two difficult marriages and a serious injury, Patsy wrote out her will in longhand giving responsibility for her children and most of her assets, including a portrait of herself, to her mother who had been able to take similar responsibility for her own life. This proved prophetic when shortly thereafter, in 1963, she was killed in a plane crash. Her music remains popular today and she has been memorialized in a 1985 movie entitled *Sweet Dreams* after a song released after her death.

SOURCE:
Margaret Tone, *Patsy: The Life and Times of Patsy Cline* (New York: HarperCollins, 1994).

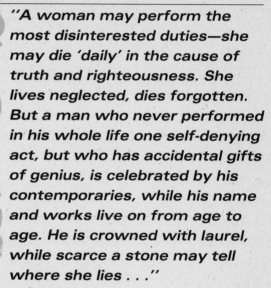

FAMOUS CHILD:	Louisa May Alcott
MOTHER'S NAME:	Abigail May "Abba" Alcott
MAMA SAID:	*"A woman may perform the most disinterested duties—she may die 'daily' in the cause of truth and righteousness. She lives neglected, dies forgotten. But a man who never performed in his whole life one self-denying act, but who has accidental gifts of genius, is celebrated by his contemporaries, while his name and works live on from age to age. He is crowned with laurel, while scarce a stone may tell where she lies . . ."*

*A*bba's discouraged lament, after years of caring for her family and worrying about finances, went far in motivating Louisa to literary heights. Throughout her life, Louisa wrote expansively on woman's

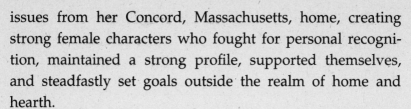

issues from her Concord, Massachusetts, home, creating strong female characters who fought for personal recognition, maintained a strong profile, supported themselves, and steadfastly set goals outside the realm of home and hearth.

Louisa's father, Bronson, spent most of his life deeply involved in educational philosophy, having started a school in a barn on his property in Concord, and for a time involving his family in a utopian community called "Fruitlands." As visionary as he may have been, his efforts provided little financial support for the Alcotts, and created extra work for Abigail. She and her daughters were left to deal with the everyday problems. With a responsibility modeled by Abigail Alcott, Louisa May set out to write a popular, and therefore more lucrative novel, *Little Women*. It was this literary effort that saved the family from financial ruin.

In addition to her literary success, Louisa May demonstrated even further responsibility by volunteering as a nurse in the Civil War in 1862, earning, according to her biographer, Martha Saxton, forty cents a day for her efforts. She wrote of her experiences in *Hospital Sketches*. Abigail

Alcott, always close to her daughter, Louisa May, was a perfect model of responsibility.

SOURCE:
Martha Saxton, *Louisa May: A Modern Biography of Louisa May Alcott* (Boston: Houghton Mifflin Co., 1977).

FAMOUS CHILD:	**Harry Houdini (Ehrich Weiss)**
MOTHER'S NAME:	**Mother Weiss**
MAMA SAID:	*"Nu, so from this you should make a living, my son?"*

*T*he wizard of magic, Harry Houdini, was born Ehrich Weiss in a ghetto of Budapest, Hungary, in 1874. His father, rabbi and scholar Mayer Samuel Weiss, and his family emigrated to Wisconsin, then to New York City, shortly after Ehrich's birth. Ehrich was the third child of six in a close, loving hard-working family before the turn of the century, who were proud to be Americans.

After Dr. Weiss died in 1892, the support of his mother and sisters was left to Houdini and his brothers. According to biographer William Lindsay Gresham, Houdini showed his responsibility early on, promising his mother that one day he would "pour a stream of gold pieces in her lap." Houdini and his kid brother Theodore "practiced rope-tie escapes on the roof of their East 69th Street house." Theodore would "spend hours tying Harry and Harry would spend even more strenuous hours wriggling out." This behavior mystified their responsible mother because "never in all the history of the Weiss family (which produced rabbis and Talmud scholars) had anyone senselessly allowed himself to be tied up with clothesline."

These disciplined rehearsals soon paid off in a big way as Houdini went on to fascinate the world with his magical tricks while supporting his family most successfully. After Houdini's death, his body was returned to New York City in "the great bronze coffin of his underwater burial challenge, and in it a packet of his mother's letters served him as a pillow."

SOURCE:
William Lindsay Gresham, *Houdini: The Man Who Walked Through Walls* (New York: Henry Holt and Co., 1959).

Self-discipline

Christa McAuliffe
Dwight D. Eisenhower
Ginger Rogers
Albert Einstein
Marie Antoinette
Jimmy Carter
Dale Carnegie
Tom Seaver
Henry Ford
Nathaniel Hawthorne
Thomas Edison
Martina Navratilova
William Gates
Margaret Thatcher
George Gershwin

Self-discipline

A person who possesses self-discipline has the willpower to accomplish or succeed. Plato's Socrates wisely observed, "A man should be temperate and master of himself and ruler of his own passions and pleasures." Self-discipline is defined as "the correction or government of oneself for the sake of improvement." As Alfred, Lord Tennyson wrote in "Oenone" in 1832,

Self-reverence, self-knowledge, self-control,
These three alone lead life to sovereign power.

Disciplined people control their behavior. Ida Eisenhower observed that her young son had a hot temper. In a house of seven sons, conflicts were inevitable. She knew that for young Dwight to succeed in life, he would have to "conquer his own soul." Ike remembered this advice as one of the best lessons of his life. Mary Ford admonished her young son Henry "life can't be all fun." Henry learned this lesson well, invented a disciplined method of building automobiles known as the assembly line, and produced thousands of basic, black, Model-T Fords.

Self-discipline is also an ability to control one's thoughts. Lela McMath taught her daughter to discipline herself and mentally focus on improving her own skills rather than comparing herself to others. This self-mastery enabled her daughter Ginger Rogers to soar professionally and delight the world with her dancing skill, unencumbered by negative thoughts.

A disciplined life is often one based on practice in order to attain excellence. According to the first-century B.C. maxim of Publilius Syrus, "Practice is the best of all instructors," which is paraphrased in the biblical proberb, "Practice makes perfect." Encouraged by their mothers, Nathaniel Hawthorne spent countless hours each day happily immersed in books; Martina Navratilova spent her childhood hitting tennis balls; Albert Einstein practiced the violin for seven years before seeing the structural relationship between music and mathematics.

In each of these stories, a mother inspired her child to achieve excellence by learning self-control and self-mastery. These children, having attained self-discipline, experienced the freedom that came with their success.

FAMOUS CHILD:	Christa McAuliffe
MOTHER'S NAME:	Grace Corrigan
MAMA SAID:	*"Christa McAuliffe is a hero, a real hero, but perhaps not for the reasons you might think. She is not a hero because of her selection as the first ordinary citizen to venture into space. She is not a hero because she provided us with a wonderful role model. Rather, she is a real hero because long before the teacher-in-space program was ever thought of, she overcame many of life's ordinary obstacles and became a worthy person."*

Christa McAuliffe—a 1970 graduate of Framingham State College in Massachusetts, wife, mother, high-school teacher, and resident of Concord, New Hampshire—was the first private citizen selected to travel into space. On January 28, 1986, with millions all over the world watching, the space shuttle *Challenger* exploded, taking the lives of all seven crew members.

Christa fashioned herself after her mother, Grace Corrigan, a self-disciplined woman of compassion and community spirit. Grace taught nursery school and served in several church groups. She was active in local politics, started a PTA chapter, and organized a Brownie troupe that launched Christa's career in the Girl Scouts. In her spare time, Grace painted in a makeshift studio at home.

Christa achieved her goals throughout her life by modeling herself after her mother's extraordinary self-discipline and commitment to family and community, which culminated not only in her becoming a worthy person but in her courageous and determined desire to become the first teacher in space. Biographer Robert T. Hohler adds, "Even new frontiers tempted Christa at an early age. She seized every opportunity to stray toward the rocks on the edge of the harbor or the tall buildings of the Boston skyline."

Clearly remembered is the self-discipline, inspiration,

and courage that one dedicated, enthusiastic teacher gave to her classroom throughout her seven-month preparation for a new frontier—the *Challenger* voyage.

SOURCE:
Robert T. Hohler, *I Touch the Future: The Story of Christa McAuliffe* (New York: Random House, 1986).

| MOTHER'S NAME: | Ida Stover Eisenhower |
| MAMA SAID: | *"He who conquereth his own soul is greater than he who taketh a city."* |

$\mathfrak{M}$rs. Eisenhower said this after Ike's brother gave him a beating with a hickory switch, after which Dwight was, in her words, "at odds with the world." For the young Eisenhower—who grew up with six brothers in a small house in Abeline, Kansas, that had "less floor space than my Pentagon office"—conflict was constant. The combination of cramped quarters and young Eisenhower's hot temper was a volatile mix.

Eisenhower remembered this particular disciplining as

"one of the most valuable moments of my life," observing in his autobiography sixty-seven years later that "to this day I make it a practice to avoid hating anyone. If someone's been guilty of despicable actions, especially toward me, I try to forget him."

Eisenhower, of course, went on to "taketh" many cities from the Nazis as Commander-in-Chief of Allied forces in World War II and became president in 1952. When, as president, he faced a number of media attacks regarding a particular incident, and an aide asked him how he had acquired the self-discipline to ignore attacks, he replied it was from his mother, "the happiest person" he had ever known.

On May 1, 1962, on what would have been his mother's one-hundredth birthday, he dedicated the Dwight D. Eisenhower Presidential Library in Abeline, Kansas. He told the crowd that Ida's sons "would like today to think that she knows that they still revere her teaching, her strength, her refusal ever to admit defeat in small or great things."

SOURCE:
Michael Beschloss, *Eisenhower: A Centennial Life* (New York: Harper-Collins, 1990).

FAMOUS CHILD:	Ginger Rogers (Virginia Katherine McMath)
MOTHER'S NAME:	Lela (Mackey) Owens McMath
MAMA SAID:	*"Never compare yourself disparagingly with another or strive to be better than another individual. Gratefully recognize your own worth as His uniquely individual idea, for you must love the other fellow with the same gratitude for his God-reflected qualities."*

Ginger Rogers was already an accomplished vaudeville singer and dancer by age fourteen. She and her mother, Lela, were on the road in St. Louis when Ginger began doing comedy skits and "happy songs and snappy chatter." The act became so popular that she landed a well-paying job with Chicago bandleader Paul Ash. But Ginger soon felt a rivalry developing between her and the band's popular singer, Peggy Brenier. Lela (who wrote all of Ginger's material) saw the potential conflict as an opportunity for Ginger to "learn the right attitude toward competition." After briefly thinking about her mother's advice, Ginger "stopped worrying about Peggy Brenier and began working with Paul Ash."

Once the disciplined Ginger changed her attitude and focused on what Paul wanted her to do, she was free from such negative comparisons. Ginger went on to give Oscar-winning performances in *Top Hat* and *Kitty Foyle*, while forging a career that spanned many decades. Ginger, who died in 1995, dedicated her 1991 autobiography to her mother:

> To my loving and beautiful mother Mackey—a perfectionist, a writer, a painter, a poet.

SOURCE:
Ginger Rogers, *Ginger: My Story* (New York: HarperCollins, 1991).

FAMOUS CHILD:	**Albert Einstein**
MOTHER'S NAME:	**Pauline Koch Einstein**
MAMA . . .	*insisted that he take music lessons.*

*A*lbert Einstein was born in the German city of Ulm, on the banks of the Danube River. His mother, Pauline, daughter of a Stuttgart grain merchant, had a pervasive love of German literature, philosophy, and music. Young Albert, shy and deliberate, was not fluent in the language until the age of nine, suggesting to recent scholars that he may have been dyslexic. This worried his parents who were told by their son's headmaster in response to a question about which profession their son should adopt that "It doesn't matter; he'll never make a success of anything."

When Albert was just six years old, his mother insisted that he take violin lessons. He dutifully learned his lessons "by rote rather than inspiration," according to biographer Ronald Clark, and "seven years passed before he was aroused by Mozart into an awareness of the mathematical structure of music." While Einstein's interest was not matched by his performance ability, Clark states that "an early hint of his future genius came from his ferocious concentration on the task to be done and his determination that nothing should be allowed to distract him from it." When stymied by a mathematical problem, Einstein often took refuge in music. He once remarked that "Music has no effect on research work, but both are born of the same source and complement each other through the satisfaction they bestow." Pauline Koch, by quietly and persistently exposing her son to music lessons, built in her son a disciplined approach not only to music, but also to the study of mathematics.

SOURCE:
Ronald W. Clark, *Einstein: The Life and Times* (New York and Cleveland: World Publishing, 1971).

FAMOUS CHILD:	Marie Antoinette
MOTHER'S NAME:	Maria Theresa
MAMA SAID:	*"The only thing I am afraid of is that you may sometimes be backward in saying your prayers, and in your reading; and may consequently grow negligent and slothful. Fight against these faults. . . . Do not forget your mother who, though far away, will continue to watch over you until her last breath."*

$\mathfrak{M}$aria Theresa, Empress of Austria, disciplined ruler and loving mother of twelve, had good cause to worry about her ninth child and youngest daughter, born in 1755. At the age of fourteen, Marie Antoinette was about to marry Louis XVI, the grandson of King Louis XV, linking the Hapsburg family of Austria with the Bourbon family of France, but, according to biographer Stefan Zweig, she was "immature, frivolous, and somewhat flighty."

Maria, hoping to reverse some of these unflattering qualities, hired tutors, hoping to educate her spirited, undisciplined daughter. Finally, before her marriage, Maria drew up a formal list of her advice, which Marie Antoinette was directed to read "on the 21st of each month." Upon the death of Louis XV, young Marie Antoinette became Queen of France, continuing her undisciplined behavior and flaunting every convention. By 1780, Maria Theresa died, despairing for her daughter.

During the French Revolution, Marie Antoinette's sheltered life was transformed. Her royal family was stripped of power, captured, and imprisoned. After the death of her mother, as her husband and children were taken from her, and she was under the threat of the guillotine, Marie Antoinette finally found the self-discipline, courage, and nobility to follow the advice of her disciplined mother, inspiring, finally, the admiration of her followers.

Now, however, it was too late. The Queen of France,

Marie Antoinette, went to her death by guillotine on October 16, 1793 in the Place de la Révolution in Paris at the age of thirty-seven.

SOURCES:

Stefan Zweig, *Marie Antoinette* (New York: Viking Press, 1933).

Manuel Komroff and Odette Komroff, *Marie Antoinette* (New York: Julian Messner, 1967).

FAMOUS CHILD:	James Earl "Jimmy" Carter, Jr.
MOTHER'S NAME:	Lillian Carter
MAMA SAID:	*"Do the best you can with what you have and don't worry about criticism."*

*L*illian Carter, who the *Washington Post* called "the nation's grandmother," lived an independent life in Plains, Georgia. She spent much time alone, according to biographers Bruce Mazlish and Edwin Diamond, which is "not too surprising, given the fact that the Carters were one of the two white families around Archery [Georgia]." She was an avid reader, having spoken of her "orgies of reading" and remembers that she was "never one to be running in and out of people's homes. She spent many long hours nursing black sharecroppers with Dr. Sam Wise, who would treat them for nothing if Lillian would "nurse them through the critical part for nothing." In 1966 at the age of sixty-eight, Lillian joined the Peace Corps, serving in India. The colorful, self-disciplined, and productive Lillian Carter learned early on that one could only "do the best you can with what you have." If criticism followed, so be it.

Jimmy Carter exemplified his mother's disciplined and productive life as he studied, entered a Navy career, ran for the Georgia senate in 1962, and subsequently ran for and won the governorship and presidency. Following his presidency, Jimmy became deeply involved with Habitat for Humanity, and founded the Carter Center in Atlanta, Georgia— dedicated to supporting peace through conflict mediation throughout the world.

SOURCE:

Bruce Mazlish and Edwin Diamond, *Jimmy Carter: An Interpretive Biography (New York: Simon & Schuster, 1979).*

FAMOUS CHILD:	**Dale Carnegie**
MOTHER'S NAME:	**Amanda Elizabeth Carnegie**
MAMA SAID:	*"I would rather hear the clods of earth rattling down on your coffin than to see you soil yourself with such filthy pawns of the devil."*

*D*ale Carnegie's youth was spent on farms in Missouri where his father, James William Carnagey (Carnagey became Carnegie later in Dale's life), "for all his industrious enterprise," write Giles Kemp and Edward Claflin, "was consistently down on his luck." The family weathered floods, poverty, dust storms, failure of crops, and plummeting prices on the Chicago commodities market.

In spite of these difficulties, the family maintained the strict moral principles of their Methodist Episcopal Church.

Dale's mother Amanda made this firm declaration upon discovering her sons playing with a deck of cards. The discipline was strict, to be sure, but the strength Dale derived from it permitted him, as a student at Warrensburg, Missouri Teachers College, to persevere despite failing to win dozens of speaking contests. Finally, when Dale won the prestigious debating contest in his senior year, he had some hope that his life might be less grueling and difficult than his parents' lives had been.

Dale Carnegie influenced millions with his 1936 book *How to Win Friends and Influence People,* one of the best-selling books of all time, which gives great emphasis to the self-discipline learned from his mother. Years after his parents' death, in a speech at Dr. Norman Vincent Peale's Marble Collegiate Church, he stated, "My parents gave me no money or financial inheritance, but they gave me something of much greater value, the blessing of faith and a sturdy character."

SOURCE:
Giles Kemp and Edward Claflin, *Dale Carnegie: The Man Who Influenced Millions* (New York: St. Martin's Press, 1989).

FAMOUS CHILD:	Tom Seaver
MOTHER'S NAME:	Betty Seaver
MAMA'S . . .	*philosophy was . . . If you tried hard enough and persevered long enough, you could achieve any goal.*

The future Hall of Fame baseball pitcher Tom Seaver never had trouble understanding the message of self-discipline that was first delivered to him by his mother when she read her young son the children's classic *The Little Engine That Could*. In this story a little steam engine struggles to climb a mountain, all the while saying, "I think I can, I think I can, I think I can." When the little train crosses the mountain, the engine proudly states "I thought I could, I thought I could."

Tom's mom was there with a message of perseverance and self-discipline many times during his baseball-playing years. Starting at age eight, when he was not allowed to play in Little League, she advised him to keep practicing. When he was not drafted by the major leagues after a successful high-school career, she advised him to go to college. Later, when the professional contract he signed after graduation from the University of Southern California was invalidated, she helped him wait out the process until he was eventually given an opportunity to be included in a special selection process.

Guided by this message of self-discipline, Tom, like the little engine, was known for his ability to believe in himself. Tom's athletic discipline enabled him to avoid injury during an eighteen-year major-league career. He won three hundred eleven games, won the Cy Young Award three times, and was named to the Baseball Hall of Fame in 1992.

SOURCE:
Gene Schoor, *Seaver: A Biography* (Chicago: Contemporary Books, 1986).

FAMOUS CHILD:	Henry Ford
MOTHER'S NAME:	Mary Litogot Ford
MAMA SAID:	*"Life cannot be all fun—you must earn the right to play."*

Born a first son of four children, Henry spent much of his childhood with a "mechanical curiosity and attitude" and was always "tinkering." According to biographer Allan Nevins, "whenever new toys came into the Ford home someone was sure to exclaim: 'Don't let Henry see them! He'll take them apart!'" At an early age, Henry Ford learned that self-discipline and persistence helped him accomplish things that other children couldn't accomplish.

Henry Ford was born to Irish immigrants in 1863 near Dearborn, Michigan, not far from Detroit. Henry's mother, Mary, died after giving birth to her eighth child in 1876, devastating the large and close family. As a young child, Henry "saw a steam engine proceeding under its own power. Thus the possibility of an engine being used as a self-propelled vehicle was implanted in Henry's mind, to haunt it and fire his imagination for years to come."

Years later, with a self-discipline developed in childhood, Henry Ford invested twenty-eight thousand dollars in cash and became an automobile pioneer known throughout the world.

In a 1928 interview with Edgar A. Guest, Henry said, "I have tried to live my life as my mother would have wished." Even his mother would have agreed that with his hard work and self-discipline, he had "earned the right to play."

SOURCE:
Allan Nevins, *Ford: The Times, The Man, The Company* (New York: Charles Scribner's Sons, 1954).

FAMOUS CHILD:	Nathaniel Hawthorne
MOTHER'S NAME:	Elizabeth Manning Hawthorne
MAMA SAID:	*"He acquired the habit of constant reading."*

athaniel Hawthorne was born in 1804 in Salem, Massachusetts. His mother, Elizabeth, spent her days awaiting the return of her mariner husband, who finally did not return and died at sea when young Nathaniel was three years old. Elizabeth, described as very bright, seldom received guests, spent evenings in her garden, and in later years took meals in her room alone, living the regulated, disciplined life of a New England widow.

Before Nathaniel was seven, he experienced the deaths of his father, his maternal grandfather Manning, and an uncle. Death dominated his early years and left him a solitary young boy who read voraciously, admitted to delicate health, and had a "grievous disinclination to go to school." At the age of nine, he was hit while playing "bat and ball" and spent the next fourteen months incapacitated but happy, lying on the floor reading. Young Nathaniel lamented, "Why was I not a girl that I might have been pinned all my life to my mother's apron?"

It wasn't until he left the confines of his solitary, disciplined life at home that Nathaniel Hawthorne flourished as a student and writer at Bowdoin in Maine, graduating with another man of letters, Henry Wadsworth Longfellow. After graduation, Hawthorne returned home, applied a discipline learned from his New England mother, and spent, according to biographer James R. Mellow, a "decade in which he served his apprenticeship as a writer immured behind the family walls." He kept a disciplined schedule; he wrote every morning, some afternoons, and then took a walk on the beach, or a dip in the ocean before returning home.

According to biographer Edwin Haviland Miller, Hawthorne was "always an observant rather than a participant" in life, which helped him collect more than enough observations for his literary works. What he didn't learn by observing, he learned by the "habit of constant reading," related his mother when Nathaniel was young. Much of his fiction, such as the *Scarlet Letter, The Marble Faun, The House of Seven Gables,* was centered around Salem, his "dwelling place" for most of his forty-six years.

SOURCES:

Edwin Haviland Miller, *Salem Is My Dwelling Place: A Life of Nathaniel Hawthorne* (University of Iowa Press, 1991).

James R. Mellow, *Nathaniel Hawthorne: In His Times* (Boston: Houghton Mifflin, 1980).

FAMOUS CHILD:	Thomas Alva Edison
MOTHER'S NAME:	Nancy Elliot Edison
MAMA SAID:	*"Will you quit worrying about better ways to light the house and go get me some stove wood. You're not going to blow up the world this afternoon."*

Thomas Edison was born in Milan, Ohio, in 1847, and later resided in Port Huron, Michigan. This quote by Edison's mother, Nancy, illustrates his early mechanical focus, which often interfered with the more practical events of everyday life. Despite his intense curiosity (he once set fire to his father's barn to see what it would do), young Edison had difficulties with school. Nancy, who had been a teacher before her marriage, withdrew her son after only three months of formal insruction and taught him herself. She encouraged his questions, and introduced him to classics such as Gibbon's *Decline and Fall of the Roman Empire*. Her disciplined approach to Tom's education led to his extensive reading in the field of science at age nine. His mother did all she could to stimulate his scientific interest, often reading aloud to him and shedding light on the knotty problems he presented to her. Edison said of her, "She was the most enthusiastic champion a boy ever had, and I determined right then that I would be worthy of her and show her that her confidence was not misplaced."

She played a major role in raising her son to be self-reliant and self-supporting. The famous inventor, who took out 1,093 patents, is credited by many for leading us into a second industrial revolution based on electricity rather than transportation. Edison is now regularly ranked with Lincoln, Roosevelt, Washington, and Franklin in opinion polls of the greatest Americans.

According to Edison scholar Wyn Wachhorst, Nancy Edison is generally credited for teaching him to "seek security in what he could acquire by his industry and conserve by his thrift." Her support, according to Edison, "was the making of me. She was so true, so sure of me; and I felt that I had someone to live for, someone I must not disappoint."

SOURCES:

Wyn Wachhorst, *Thomas Alva Edison: An American Myth* (Cambridge: MIT Press, 1981).

Mabel Bartlett and Sophia Baker, *Mothers: Makers of Men* (New York: Exposition Press, 1952).

FAMOUS CHILD:	Martina Navratilova
MOTHER'S NAME:	Jana Semanska Navratilova
MAMA SAID:	*"Sports are good for young women. It's good to compete, good to run, good to sweat, good to get dirty, good to feel tired and healthy and refreshed."*

artina, known for her athleticism on the tennis court and her aggressive play marked by powerful serves and forehand volleys, noted in her memoirs that her athletic mother, Jana, was her role model. In her autobiography Martina states that her mother was a "full-time athlete, full-time worker, full-time mother." Her encouragement of fitness and athletic pursuit within the highly disciplined life of a career mother, fostered Martina's own athletic self-discipline.

While Jana's own mother was a tennis star in Czechoslovakia, Jana had turned her primary attention to skiing because of pressure put on her by her father to emulate her mother. She continued, however, to focus on her own athleticism, which carried over to her daughter. Martina stated: "We had no idea of tomboys—there's no word for it in the Czech language. Women played sports and had families and jobs. That simple. My mother was my role model."

When Martina was still young, her mother was married a second time to Mirek Navratil, who helped Jana rediscover tennis. He became Jana's regular tennis partner and, along with Jana, encouraged young Martina to actively pursue her own tennis interest. They retained a renowned tennis coach for Martina when she was nine.

In 1975 at age eighteen, Martina defected from then Communist Czechoslovakia. In 1984, in a remarkable testimony to her self-discipline, she won seventy-four straight matches, an all-time record.

SOURCE:
Martina Navratilova with George Vecsey, *Martina* (New York: Alfred A. Knopf, 1985).

FAMOUS CHILD:	**William Henry Gates**
MOTHER'S NAME:	**Mary Maxwell Gates**
MAMA . . .	*was anxious that Bill "learn good study habits, get some discipline in his life, not sit around thinking all the time, but that he prepare himself to develop some kind of a good school record so that he could go to any college that he wanted to attend."*

𝔐ary Maxwell Gates knew that her son, the future chairman of Microsoft, was very bright. By the age of nine he had already read the entire World Book Encyclopedia. Trey, as his parents called him, routinely chided them for "insufficient intellectum." He spent a lot of time in quiet contemplation and when urged by his parents to be ready when they were going somewhere, would often reply "I'm thinking."

Mary said, "Bill was a person who was independent from the time he was seven or eight years old. We were not controlling his life in any way. We were just trying to hold things together and have as much influence as possible."

Finally in 1968, when Bill was thirteen, his school got an ASR33 Teletype machine which intrigued the future Microsoft founder. He quickly learned what made it work and when the school was later connected to a DEC PDP10 computer through the efforts of a University of Washington Computer Center group that called themselves C-Cubed, Gates had found his niche. It was like "manna from heaven" to Bill when the group offered free computer time to Seattle high-school students willing to help out with programming. Applying his earlier motherly message of self-discipline to his newfound interest, Bill immersed himself in C-Cubed, often sneaking out late at night to go to the computer center. His mother often wondered why "it was so hard for him to get up in the morning."

Bill did fulfill his mother's wish that he go to college. He enrolled at Harvard, but soon left to start a software company. Bill did return to Harvard and completed six semesters before making his software business a full-time effort. The rest is history as Bill Gates's company, Microsoft, developed products like DOS and Windows, which proved to be the missing link between the personal computer and its widespread use.

SOURCE:
Stephen Manes and Paul Andrews, *Gates* (New York: Simon & Schuster, 1993).

FAMOUS CHILD:	Lady Margaret Roberts Thatcher
MOTHER'S NAME:	Beatrice Stephenson Roberts
MAMA SAID:	*"The worse that can be said about someone is, 'They lived up to the hilt.' "*

The future prime minister of Great Britain, Margaret Thatcher, learned from her parents the importance of thrift and self-discipline, which turned out to be trademarks of her political philosophy. She once said, "both by instinct and upbringing I was always a 'true blue conservative.' "

Margaret's shopkeeper family lived above their grocery shop in the small Lincolnshire town of Grantham. Since they were always on duty to respond to a neighbor's need,

Margaret recalled that "life over the shop" was more than a phrase to the Roberts family. In her book, *The Path to Power*, Lady Thatcher states that she "learned from her mother just what it meant to cope with a household so that everything worked like clockwork even though she had to spend so many hours behind the counter." Margaret notes her mother found time to make clothes, cook in the most economical way, and consistently sought "excellent value for the money." She added, "Nothing in our household was ever wasted."

Mrs. Thatcher recalled that entertainment was permitted if it demanded something of you rather than allowing you to be a mere spectator. To her Methodist parents, reality was in the here and now and idleness was a sin. Such thinking was exemplified in a stanza from an eighteenth-century Henry Wadsworth Longfellow poem which was typical of those read and valued by her family:

> The heights by great men reached and kept
> Were not attained by sudden flight
> But they, while their companions slept,
> Were toiling upward in the night.

Margaret often used these verses in speeches during her political career which began with election to the House of Parliament in 1959 at age thirty-four and which culminated with her election as the first woman prime minister of Great Britain, from 1979 to 1990. Her conservative political values and disciplined manner of applying them were rooted in lessons learned from her mother's lifestyle.

When Beatrice died in 1960, Margaret credited her with being the "rock of family stability" for her efforts to manage the household, run the shop when needed, entertain, support her husband's public life as the town's mayoress, and do volunteer work for charities. She concluded that she had inherited from her "my ability to organize . . . so many different duties of an active life."

SOURCE:
Margaret Thatcher, *The Path to Power* (New York: HarperCollins, 1995).

FAMOUS CHILD:	George Gershwin
MOTHER'S NAME:	Rose Gershwin
MAMA . . .:	*was ambitious and purposeful, and wanted George to get ahead in the world—and this meant to do well in school.*

Mr. and Mrs. Gershwin had come from Russia in the 1890s to the Lower East Side in New York City to escape the czars and find opportunity. Rose Gershwin was ambitious and kept a sharp eye on the financial side of her husband's business, while fervently hoping that her children would work hard in school. George's older brother, Ira, got good grades but George didn't do well in school and spent much time playing hooky and fighting. His mother just couldn't understand how young

George was ever going to get ahead in the world without enough discipline to get an education.

George was not exposed to music at home; phonographs were too expensive, and radios had not yet been invented. He often taunted other children he called "Maggies," who took their music lessons seriously and weren't as tough or athletic. Boys, according to Rose Gershwin, should be playing outside or doing things. Girls could be involved in music.

One day George was outside on the playground playing ball while a concert was taking place inside his school. Soon the melodic strains of Dvorak's *Humoresque* played on the violin came wafting through the air, according to him later, "like a flashing revelation of beauty." George just had to meet this virtuoso. Gershwin reminisced about Max, the young violinist many years later, "From the first moment we became friends. Max opened the world of music to me." George spent days at his friend's home, learning to play their piano, constantly talking about music, experimenting with chords and harmony, and growing more and more excited. The self-discipline that George was unable to apply to his studies was directed toward his love for music.

In 1910, when George was twelve, Rose Gershwin purchased a second-hand upright, for the business had gone well and her sister had bought one that year. "No sooner had it come through the window and been backed up against the wall, than I was at the keys," related George later. "Where had George, the son who got bad marks in school and never concentrated on anything, learned music? Now he was a 'Maggie' too!" related biographer Robert Rushmore. The whole family was impressed.

At the age of fifteen, George left school to pursue his dream of a career in music. He had gotten a job as a Tin Pan Alley song plugger for Remick's, a music publisher, for fifteen dollars a week. Soon, he realized that he could write songs as well as those he was plugging. His song, *"Red Hot Mama,"* was published when he was eighteen and sung by Sophie Tucker, beginning a song-writing career, often in collaboration with his brother Ira, that lit up Broadway for many years. Rose Gershwin, now proud of her disciplined young son, was always amazed, however, that someone could become so successful by "just writing music."

SOURCE:
Robert Rushmore, *The Life of George Gershwin* (New York: Macmillan Co., 1966).

INDEX

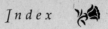

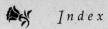

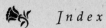

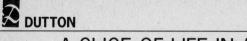 DUTTON PLUME

A SLICE OF LIFE IN AMERICA

☐ **MID-LIFE CONFIDENTIAL** *The Rock Bottom Remainders Tour America with Three Chords and an Attitude.* **Edited by Dave Marsh.** In 1992, fifteen of America's most popular writers—including Stephen King, Amy Tan, Dave Barry, and Barbara Kingsolver—left their day jobs for life on the rock 'n' roll road. They called themselves the Rock Bottom Remainders and spent two weeks barnstorming the East Coast—staying up late, eating junk food, traveling by bus, and actually trying to play and sing before paying audiences, massacring rock 'n' roll classics everywhere. (274591—$12.95)

☐ **BEHIND THE OSCAR** *The Secret History of the Academy Awards* **by Anthony Holden.** At last, the full story of the winners, the losers, the scandals, and the whispers can be told. You'll find out why some of the greatest names in movie history were ignored, and how others were destroyed by the Oscar jinx. Complete with a multitude of award lists and dozens of photos. (271312—$15.95)

☐ **SUMMER OF LOVE** *The Inside Story of LSD, Rock & Roll, Free Love and High Times in the Wild West* **by Joel Selvin.** In the late 1960s and 1970s, the West Coast was the epicenter of rock music. Drawing on more than 200 interviews with all the major players, including Jerry Garcia, Grace Slick, Steve Miller, and David Crosby, the author has assembled the first complete history of this era—a visual "Psychedelic Babylon." "A backstage pass to the wildest, boldest, scariest era in American rock and roll."—Carl Hiaasen (274079—$12.95)

☐ **THE TWENTYSOMETHING AMERICAN DREAM** *A Cross-Country Quest for a Generation* **by Michael Lee Cohen.** This groundbreaking collection of interviews goes beyond the sound bites to reveal the thoughts and souls of Americans in their twenties. This important book surpasses the generalizations to show that much of the negative media hype is unsubstantiated, and that twentysomethings make up a fascinating, diverse group confronting the challenges of the future. (272300—$10.95)

Prices slightly higher in Canada.